the Seven love letters of Jesus

PASTOR STEVE BERGER
WITH WAYNE HASTINGS

The Seven Love Letters of Jesus
© 2009 by Steve Berger, Senior Pastor Grace Chapel

Printed in the United States

Cover and Interior design: Matt Dolan
Editor: Jennifer Hesse

ISBN 978-1-936355-00-6

CONTENTS

INTRODUCTION

*F*riends, in the next six chapters we are going to study seven letters the Lord Jesus lovingly wrote to seven churches located in seven cities in Asia (modern-day Turkey). These letters were preserved for us by the apostle John in the Book of Revelation. John heard Jesus' words, and he wrote them not only to the seven churches but to us today.

There is tremendous meaning and instruction for Christians today in these seven love letters. In the letter to the church at Pergamos, Jesus said:

> "He who has an ear, let him hear what the Spirit says to the churches. To him who overcomes I will give some of the hidden manna to eat"
>
> Revelation 2:17

Before beginning this study, there are a few important things to know and remember.

HAVE AN EAR TO HEAR

First, Jesus did not write these letters to make you feel guilty, lousy, or down on yourself. He wrote these letters in love to people He loves. In the letters, He addresses some things He approves of and also points out things He does not condone. He speaks with authority, but also in love. In the end, Jesus wants all of us. He doesn't want anything to distract us from His love, His plan, or His power. Sometimes He must point out to us where we've strayed and how far we've gone away from Him. In these letters, Jesus lovingly brings us back, and all He asks is that we have an ear to hear.

Be prepared to listen to His voice as you read and study these love letters.

BE AN OVERCOMER

Jesus wants us to overcome. He sees us in our self-propelled lives doing whatever to get along and missing the bigger picture that He's there for us. He wrote these letters to move us to become less dependent on everything but Him—and to do that, He encourages us to be overcomers.

Overcomers are not suddenly perfect people. Overcomers are not just okay with going to church and sitting nicely in the chairs, ready to shake somebody's hand or sing the next verse kind of people. Overcomers are people who know they have hurdles in their lives and know they need Jesus to get them over them. Overcomers are people, like you and me, who deeply desire to hear Jesus' voice and move away from the past. Overcomers choose to move on with their hand in Jesus' hand—one step at a time.

Jacob was an overcomer. In Genesis 32 he fought with an Angel. In verse 25 the Angel touched Jacob's hip and dislocated it. When the Angel tried to leave, Jacob would not let go until the Angel blessed him. Jacob struggled with God, and he was renamed Israel because he "struggled with God and with men, and . . . prevailed" (*Gen. 32:28*).

Jacob overcame and received a new name. He also walked with a limp, and like many of us who have visible or invisible "limps," he overcame, he prevailed, and he learned to trust God.

ENJOY THE MANNA

In the desert during the Exodus, the Israelites were given the gift of manna. It fell from heaven and met every dietary need they had. After a while, however, they grew tired of the manna. They whined for other things—things that in the past never came close to satisfying them as the manna satisfied.

Friends, there are some tremendous lessons for us in these seven love letters. They are lessons directly from Jesus, and they are lessons that will meet every need we have. They are hard lessons, but they are the best lessons we can learn.

Don't get weary or tired as we move along. Trust God to help you see, with new eyes, some things about yourself and about your church that are distractions from totally trusting Him and knowing Him fully. Don't get tired of this precious manna, but enjoy it, even when it's hard.

Jesus' desire is for you to know, obey, and trust Him. Jesus' desire for your church is that it will know, obey, and trust Him. It's all right here as the manna was for the Israelites. Partake of it.

DIG IN

There are six lessons in this short book and accompanying study guide. They are:

- The Letter to Ephesus - The loveless church
- The Letter to Smyrna - The persecuted church
- The Letters to Pergamos and Thyatira
  The compromising churches
- The Letter to Sardis - The dead church
- The Letter to Philadelphia - The faithful church
- The Letter to Laodicea - The lukewarm church

For each section we have included an overview of the message plus a study guide. Use each as a way to understand and apply what Jesus is saying to you and your church.

You will learn that Jesus is standing at the door and knocking. He wants to join you wherever you are. If you hear Him knocking, let Him into your life, let Him into your heart, and let Him into your mind. He's knocking. He's ready. He's there.

Open the door and let Him in. Open the door and let His words create something new and challenging within you and your church today.

Open the door.

● ● ● ● ● ● ● ● ● ● ● ● ● ● ● ● ●

Part 1

The church at Ephesus

1

PREFACE

Do you know that Jesus loves speaking to His church? In fact, it doesn't get much clearer than the passages we're going to study. Over the next few chapters, we'll discover that Jesus, very specifically, has a word for seven different churches in what is now modern-day Turkey. What's interesting is that the message wasn't just for those seven churches; it was recorded in Scripture for our benefit two thousand years later. There are aspects of these churches that are in every church today and that are in every believer on some level. There's much to glean from Jesus' message for all of us.

Typically, when we are asked to open the Book of Revelation, everyone's mind goes to things that were written from chapter 6 forward. When people think of the Book of Revelation, they think about the scary stuff, the spooky stuff, and the funky-looking beasts with horns and eyeballs all over. They think about the 144,000, the trumpet judgments, the bowl judgments, the earth being burned up, and the Battle of Armageddon and all that. Now, I don't say this irreverently at all, because all those actions and symbols and words are seriously important and seriously true. But I've got to tell you, as much as I've studied this book for years and listened to every tape on it that I can find, what concerns me and has my curiosity up more than anything has nothing to do with chapter 6 forward and has everything to do with chapters 2 and 3.

I'm more concerned today about the condition of the church and what Jesus has to say to the church than I am for all the stuff that's up for grabs and interpretation. What has my attention is what Jesus has to say to the church. And so over the next few chapters, we're going to unpack the passage of Scripture in Revelation 2—3.

We're going to carefully unpack what Jesus had to say to these seven churches, and we're going to see where it applies to our lives personally as well as in a greater context—our local church and the church at large. There's going to be some challenging stuff, but here's the good thing about when Christ challenges us: Jesus doesn't challenge us just to challenge us. He doesn't challenge us just to rattle us or make us feel guilty or convicted or beat up in some way. Jesus always challenges His church because He loves us, and when He sees us going just a bit astray, on whatever level, He loves us so much that He says, "Hey! I'm back over here. You went over there, but I'm back over here. Come back, come back, come back."

It's all because of His love. Because whom the Lord loves, He chastens. And if we'll endure that chastening, we will become partakers of His righteousness. So over the course of this book and study, we're going to hear some encouraging words, but we might also hear Jesus poking His finger at us a little bit. My personal challenge to you is, let's listen to what He says. And better yet, let's respond appropriately to what He says. Here we go!

BACKGROUND

I've got to give you some context before we jump into this study. At the time this letter was written, the church had been around for about sixty years. The church was birthed at Pentecost, and sixty years have now passed. Over those sixty years, of the remaining disciples (Judas committed suicide), ten died as martyrs for their faith as they went around traveling, preaching the gospel, and going into all the world. Now, only one remains. We know him as John the Beloved, not John the Baptist, but John the Beloved. Historically, we also know that within about the last twenty years, Jerusalem had been leveled, as Jesus said it would be in John 2. Titus, the Roman Emperor, came in and wiped it out. He leveled Jerusalem to the ground and destroyed the temple. It's never been rebuilt in two thousand years. So a lot of changes had gone on between Acts and Revelation. The new church had been persecuted, people were killed because of their faith, and yet the church grew like crazy. Why did it grow? Because the church never grows very well when all is well and at ease. The church always grows the best when it's marinating in the blood of its martyrs. That's when it grows the best. Apart from that, we just have religion. But the church always grows the best under extreme persecution.

So, John was the only disciple left, He was an old guy, in his late eighties, maybe into his nineties, and he was exiled on the is land of Patmos. Patmos is this kind of volcanic ash heap. It's run by Greece, and it's right off the coast of what we now call Turkey.

There was a message that came to John as an old man. I'm sure he wondered why he was still alive after everyone else was gone and after everything else had gone on. He went into the mouth of a cave and began to worship, and he saw something he'd never seen before—the Book of Revelation.

Let's look at Revelation 1:10–17, just to give you some of the drama and the intrigue of this. John said:

I was in the Spirit on the Lord's Day, and I heard behind me a loud voice, as of a trumpet, saying, "I am the Alpha and the Omega, the First and the Last," and, "What you see, write in a book and send it to the seven churches which are in Asia: to Ephesus, to Smyrna, to Pergamos, to Thyatira, to Sardis, to Philadelphia, and to Laodicea." Then I turned to see the voice that spoke with me. And having turned I saw seven golden lampstands, and in the midst of the seven lampstands One like the Son of Man, clothed with a garment down to the feet and girded about the chest with a golden band. His head and hair were white like wool, as white as snow, and His eyes like a flame of fire; His feet were like fine brass, as if refined in a furnace, and His voice as the sound of many waters; He had in His right hand seven stars, out of His mouth went a sharp two-edged sword, and His countenance was like the sun shining in its strength. And when I saw Him, I fell at His feet as dead. But He laid His right hand on me, saying to me, "Do not be afraid; I am the First and the Last."

Now real quick, that's the only physical description of Jesus Christ in the entire New Testament. John was praying and all of a sudden he heard this thundering voice, and when he turned around, he saw Jesus, as he just described for us. So then of course it doesn't surprise us that the next verse says, "When I saw Him, I fell at His feet as dead. But He laid His right hand on me, saying to me, 'Do not be afraid; I am the First and the Last.'"

So this account is kind of told in the context of spiritual cinematography, and in this experience Jesus instructs John to write letters to the seven churches. The first letter is Ephesus, and that's what we're going to unpack over the next few pages.

• • • • • • • • • • • • • • • • •

THE MESSAGE TO THE CHURCH AT EPHESUS

Listen to Jesus speaking in Revelation 2:1–3:

> "To the angel of the church of Ephesus write, 'These things says He who holds the seven stars in His right hand, who walks in the midst of the seven golden lampstands: "I know your works, your labor, your patience, and that you cannot bear those who are evil. And you have tested those who say they are apostles and are not, and have found them liars; and you have persevered and have patience, and have labored for My name's sake and have not become weary."'"
>
> Revelation 2:1–3

Don't you know that when they read that scroll at the church at Ephesus, and Jesus was going on and on about all the great things about them, that the church members started feeling pretty good? Wouldn't we?

That's right, we would. We have labored, we've been patient, we've endured some bad stuff—you better believe we'd be jumping up and down. There's more. We know our Bibles, too. We're testing those who say they're apostles and they're not. Man, we know those guys are liars. And talk about living right? We can't endure those who are evil, and we are morally happening—we are moral in our conduct, we are pure, we're not compromising with the world, and we're doing all that good, right Christian stuff. That's right. Preach it, Jesus!

And as they're all patting each other on the back, the reader says, "Um hum hum hum . . ." Gulp. "Boys, there's more."

"Well, what else? What's He got to say to us?"

"Well, He says . . .

'Nevertheless I have this against you, that you have left your first love. Remember therefore from where you have fallen; repent and do the first works, or else I will come to you quickly and remove your lampstand from its place—unless you repent. But this you have, that you hate the deeds of the Nicolaitans, which I also hate. He who has an ear, let him hear what the Spirit says to the churches. To him who overcomes I will give to eat from the tree of life, which is in the midst of the Paradise of God.'"

Revelation 2:4–7

You can't help but notice all the great things. They worked, they labored for Christ's name, they persevered, they didn't put up with evil, they tested false apostles, they were patient, they didn't become weary, and they hated the deeds of the Nicolaitans. Wow! What a church. So much right stuff going on:

- sound in doctrine
- active in service
- moral in conduct

Any of us would be proud to say, "I've got my membership over there." Sound in doctrine, active in service, and moral in conduct. But with so much right, Jesus still had a staggering indictment, a staggering challenge for them to consider about themselves. And He said it real plainly: "Hey you all, you have left your first love."

The honeymoon was over. Christ was actually outside of their Christianity. They asked themselves, "How could that have happened? We're doing all the right stuff. We're studying, we're not putting up with evil, we're serving in the youth ministry, we're working with kids and the homeless, and we're doing all the stuff."

"But you're doing it without Me," Jesus said.

That's why later, when we get to the letter to Laodicea, He's knocking at the door. Why is Jesus knocking on the door?

Cause He's outside. You don't knock if you're already inside. You say, "Hi!" when you're already in. You knock when you want in. But we'll get there in later chapters to come. What we have to remember first about the Ephesians is that **they left their first love.**

Second, we see that the Ephesian believers satisfied themselves in sound orthodoxy. They determined that sound doctrine, Christian service, and moral conduct was somehow enough. Maybe it had even happened slowly over the years, and they thought the ultimate goal of being a Christian was to know what they believed and why they believed it. They thought the goal was to serve the Lord and live a moral life. That became the climate of all things Christian to them. Maybe that's what they thought, but they were wrong. **They thought wrong**. And I wonder if we do today.

Third, the Ephesian church forgot that Christ was most interested in their hearts, not their hands or their heads. Beloved, it is about our hearts. It's about fond affection and adoration for the Person of Jesus, not the principles of Christianity. And it's a fine line that gets foggy sometimes. **They forgot about their hearts**.

The Ephesians forgot that above all things, the one thing that is necessary is to be in God's presence, to sit at His feet, to hear His Word, to adore Him, to make His praise glorious, and to have heartfelt, real communion with the Son of God. That's what Christianity is about. And out of the depth of that love relationship is where everything else needs to flow. If we're doing things apart from that, it's religion, it's Christianity, but it's not Jesus. And that's what Jesus said in His letter to the Ephesians. I'm sure they felt a bit convicted.

Now, sadly, there are some similarities between the Ephesians and the Pharisees, who Jesus rebuked as being whitewashed tombs (*Matt. 23:27*). These guys studied, studied, studied, and studied, but missed Jesus altogether. Do you remember what Jesus told the Pharisees who lived right and acted right and memorized right and studied right? Do you remember what He said to those guys who were so sound in doctrine? Jesus said to the Pharisees:

> "You search the Scriptures, for in them you think you have eternal life; and these are they which testify of Me. But you are not willing to come to Me that you may have life."

John 5:39, 40,

This line, beloved, is so thin that we cross it and don't even realize it. Making the point I'm about to make is so fine that I'm going to get criticized for saying the truth because it's going to be misunderstood. But I'm going to say it anyway. Bear with me. We can study the Scriptures until we are blue in the face, but if the Scriptures don't lead us to a personal encounter with Jesus Christ, we are as the Pharisees of old. I get more and more concerned about the church in general all the time because we get preoccupied with the words of God and not THE Word of God. And there is a huge difference. I'm not saying don't study. Study! Study to "present yourself approved to God, a worker who does not need to be ashamed, rightly dividing the word of truth" (*2 Timothy 2:15*). And have an answer for "everyone who asks you a reason for the hope that is in you" (*1 Pet. 3:15*)—

I preach that all the time. I'm preaching the Bible, and our church is dedicated to discipling people.

I'm not saying don't study—I'm saying study, but make sure it leads you to an encounter with Christ. Because Jesus said it is fully possible to study the Scriptures and to think that because you studied them that you have eternal life. But the Scriptures testify of Jesus, and the Ephesians weren't willing to come to Jesus for life. They satisfied themselves with print and not Person—scroll and not Savior.

Study, yes, but make sure it's taking you to Jesus. The church at Ephesus studied, they were sound in doctrine, and they stood for the truth—but they chose to leave Jesus outside. Let's make sure that we're hungering for THE Word of God and not just the words of God. You can give answers to somebody about your faith, but you miss the point if He's not real and in your heart.

It was the late, great Leonard Ravenhill who spoke of "lifeless textualism" and said, "God's problem today is not communism, nor yet Romanism, nor liberalism, nor modernism. God's problem is -- dead fundamentalism!"[1] The greatest threat to Christianity isn't liberal theology; it's not a wicked world that's going to hell in a hand basket. The greatest hindrance, the greatest stumbling block to people coming to Christ is people who are right—dead right. They are sound in doctrine, active in service, moral in conduct, **but not loving Jesus**. It's possible. I know a lot of people who will hear that and go, "Man, how could they?" I hear that and go, "God forbid me!" I want to learn from their mistakes; I don't want to make my own. And any time I study and read this letter to the Ephesians in Revelation, it's always a fresh time to say, "Let me check my heart." And here's the question: "Jesus, have I become so busy in fashioning sermons and leading the church and starting Bible studies and doing whatever it is that I do, that somehow You're outside?"

It's about doing everything for Him. Nothing—not my messages to you, not the Bible studies I lead, not the everyday ministry details—nothing is more important than getting on my knees or sitting in my shower for a half hour or forty-five minutes and just saying:

"Jesus, I love You. Thank You for what You have done in my life. Thank You for saving me, God. Thank You for being patient with me. Thank You for loving me and forgiving me and filling me with the Holy Spirit. Thank You, God, for letting me see truths in Your Word, and thank You for allowing me to share them with other people. Thank You, Jesus, for who You are. I love You. I love You, Lord. Forget all the accolades and all the stuff and the church—whatever with that. Jesus, You have arrested my heart. And whether there are five or fifty of five bajillion people, it doesn't matter. What matters, Jesus,

is that I'm loving You purposefully and passionately every single day."

We must make sure that everything we're doing, we're doing for Jesus. And at the same time, we must continue to ask: "Are we doing whatever we're doing without Jesus?" That's what we have to start thinking about and every minute checking our hearts and our minds to make sure we're letting Him into everything.

CHRIST'S LOVING REBUKE

Jesus didn't just point out the Ephesians' faults and then leave them hanging. No, He told them how to fix the problem. Jesus said, "Hey, church, I've got something that you all need to do." First, **you need to remember from where you've fallen** (*Rev. 2:5*). Remember that you've left your first love and the honeymoon is over. Remember from where you've fallen. He said, "I want you to remember and go back, go back in your mind to when we were first introduced to one another. Go back to when we were new lovers. Go back."

Take a minute yourself and think about what it was like when people asked you, "Hey, do you go to the nine or the eleven o'clock service?" and you just said, "Yes." Go back and think about what it was like when you came to church freshly understanding the grace of God, not having many answers, but knowing this: "I once was blind, but now I see." Go back to a time when you knew, deep in your heart, that Jesus loved you—and you didn't know much more than that. You remember what it was like? Coming into church and worshiping and looking around and going, "Well, I mean, I'm grateful and thankful, and I love You and all that stuff, Lord, but there, there seem to be people around me here who love You more than I do. And . . . I'm wondering what all this raising hands stuff is about. And is there a difference between one hand raised and both hands raised?!"

And so then, you know, you're there and He's saying, "I want you to remember, I want you to remember when you couldn't take it any more and when the light came on and you said to yourself, 'YES! YES! YES! Now I get it. Now I see. Man, there's people raising and clapping their hands and shouting for every silly thing under the sun. Now I see the worth and the value of raising my hands to the Son of God who saved me and gave me the hope of heaven forever. This is wonderful, Jesus. I don't know if I can pull my hands down. Lord, this is going to be embarrassing—the preacher is getting ready to preach, and I'm still standing out here with my hands up. I'm still at the altar, all the prayer people have left and gone back to their seats, and I'm still like this.'"

Remember? First love. Remember what it was like when you fell in love? You could not wait to make that phone call, you couldn't wait to receive it, and you dreaded hanging up.

"No, you hang up first."

"Not me. No, you hang up first."

"Huh uh, not me."

"I love you more than . . ."

"No, I love you more than you love me."

On and on—silly, childish, wonderful first love. Just hearing the name, wow.

"Hey, Sarah called."

"She did?!"

It was before cell phones. There was a handwritten message on some, you know, piece of rock outside or something. No text messaging back then.

"She called! Wow!"

"Hey, want to get together?"

"Tell me where and when. Absolutely I want to get together. Yeah, I know all four tires on my car are flat, but hey, I can get there. It'll drive, I'll be all right, I'm going to trust the Lord." Crazy, passionate, first love.

Jesus said, "Remember, remember, remember, church! Being doctrinally sound, active in service, and morally pure are important, but you also have to remember the heart beat." It is not Christianity—it is Christ Jesus. And He says, "Remember."

Second, **you need to remember that this problem can repeat itself**. This issue of forgetting Jesus in the midst of doing religion wasn't just the Ephesians' problem, and it wasn't just the Pharisees. It is an age-old problem, which tells me that if it repeats itself in history, it can repeat itself today.

Read Jeremiah 2:1, 2:

> "Moreover the word of the Lord came to me, saying, "Go and cry in the hearing of Jerusalem, saying, 'Thus says the Lord: "I remember you, the kindness of your youth, the love of your betrothal, when you went after Me in the wilderness, in a land not sown."
>
> Jeremiah 2:1, 2

In other words, "I remember when we got engaged." The people lost their first love.

Jesus' message of pursuing, passionate love echoes throughout the Bible: "I want you to remember Me because I remember you. I haven't forgotten you. I remember what it was like when we were young and in love. I remember when we got engaged. I remember how thrilled you were to pray and worship and talk to Me and spend time in My presence and tell other people about Me."

When you're in love, you don't forget. I don't fall out of love with Sarah. Why is it any different with Jesus?

Third, **you need to remember to share your love**. When we're in love, we talk about it. We're open and we feel free. Nobody has to tell me to talk about Sarah, but for some reason, we stop talking about Jesus. I think there are two reasons for this:

- We've stopped being fascinated, and
- We've stopped being in love with who He is.

When you love something, you're going to talk about it. I don't care if it's shredded beef tacos or almighty God—you're going to tell somebody somewhere, "This is good. I love this." There has to be something that just makes us love God and want to spend time with Him and tell others about Him. If you're not quick to speak His name, if you're not quick to share about who He is and what He can do for people, there's a chance you might have left your first love. And there's a chance that you might have to remember from where you've fallen.

CHRIST'S SIMPLE SOLUTION: REPENT

You see, beloved, repentance isn't just for the lost person who comes in off the street. It's not just for a person whose life is a wreck, of whom we would say, "Oh man, that person needs to repent." Jesus said to the church, "You need to repent; you need to turn back from the folly of your own way of doing Christianity without Christ, and you need to come back to that heart of worship, that singleness of mind and purpose."

You need to be able to say, "Lord, it's not about the ministry I do or the fact that I don't drink or smoke or cuss anymore. It's not about all these great, moral things that I do or about, you know, my great biblical understanding." It's not about that. It's about saying, "I love You—more than anything."

CHRIST'S SIMPLE INSTRUCTION: RETURN

Jesus said, "I want you to remember from where you've fallen, I want you to repent, and I want you to come back." The church's first works defined their first love, so let's go back in Scripture to the early church and where they were. We need to have that mentality and mindset of learning from their experience. There are five lessons that will help us return to our first love:

1. They were honest about their current level of experience with the Holy Spirit.

> And it happened, while Apollos was at Corinth, that Paul, having passed through the upper regions, came to Ephesus. And finding some disciples he said to them, "Did you receive the Holy Spirit when you believed?" So they said to him, "We have not so much as heard whether there is a Holy Spirit." And he said to them, "Into what then were you baptized?" So they said, "Into John's baptism."
>
> Acts 19:1–3

These people were believers; they were disciples. Paul said, "Hey, did the Holy Spirit come upon you when you first believed?" The church responded, "Hey, we've never even heard of this. We've never heard of such a thing." This passage teaches that the church needs to be honest about what the Holy Spirit is doing in their lives right now.

These Ephesian believers were honest about where they were. They admitted they had never heard of the Holy Spirit. They were taught by Apollos, and in Acts 8:18, it says that Apollos was eloquent and mighty in Scripture and taught accurately the things of the Lord. He was this great preacher, but he only knew the baptism of John. So he taught accurately the things he knew, but he didn't know about the baptism of the Holy Spirit, so he didn't teach about it. These believers were honest and said, "Hey, we don't know anything about it."

What about you? For some of you, it might be, "I don't know anything about this Holy Spirit thing." Or some of you may look back at the church you grew up in, and you were taught that the Holy Spirit isn't for today, so you don't know anything about the Holy Spirit.

Let me set the record straight. If you were told the baptism of the Holy Spirit and the power of God isn't for today, if you were told that signs and wonders don't happen anymore, you were lied to. How in the world brilliant theologians come up with this stuff, that as the world gets more and more wicked and its ungodliness gets more and more powerful, that God has stopped giving power to the church? Come on! What God and what gospel are they talking about? Are we just supposed to retreat and say, "To hell with the world. We're going to sit over here with our limited power because, you know, God doesn't do that anymore, and we live in a different dispensation"? God forbid! God forbid! If you've been told speaking in tongues is of the devil, watch out for those people. You've been lied to, and you need to get a dose of the Ghost. That's just the truth.

So be honest. If you don't know, be honest and seek the truth.

2. They were teachable and responsive to further instruction.

The early believers were willing to be instructed beyond what they had already learned. This applies to some of you who attend church and you're still not sure why. You sit in church, and the teaching makes you nervous. Maybe you've been taught things that aren't correct. You've been taught as much as your teachers were taught. You have to understand that there's more. The Ephesians were willing to be taught beyond everything else they had already learned. Acts 19:4 says, "Then Paul said, 'John indeed baptized with a baptism of repentance, saying to the people that they should believe on Him who would come after him, that is, on Christ Jesus.'"

They didn't fight it. They didn't say, "Well, Apollos never taught us about the baptism of the Holy Spirit. And if it was real, he surely would have taught us about it. So, I'm not so sure about this Paul. He's a little strange anyway, and I've heard about him. He sees visions and stuff, and so we're not going to go that route."

They didn't say any of that. They were teachable and responsive. Let me ask you, would you let the Holy Spirit take you aside and teach you the way of God more accurately? Will you allow Him to teach you things you've never been taught before, specifically about His power? Because He wants to, and He's just waiting for you.

3. They were open and receptive to the Holy Spirit.

The Ephesian believers received the Holy Spirit. They were honest about where they were, they were willing to be taught more, and they didn't resist the Holy Spirit—they received Him.

> "And when Paul had laid hands on them, the Holy Spirit came upon them, and they spoke with tongues and prophesied"
>
> Acts 19:6

The Holy Spirit came, they got a new prayer language, and they started using spiritual gifts—just like that. Imagine with me that there was a conversation that went something like this:

Paul: *"Well, all right, now here's how this works. I'm going to lay hands on you and start praying for you, and umm . . . if something happens, go with it."*

Ephesians: *"Okay, all right. We're willing to learn, we're willing to grow, we're willing to go to the next place. We're willing to be childlike—not foolish, not undiscerning—but we're ready and receptive for more of the power and the gifts of God."*

What concerns me is when I read this scripture and then see what the Bible says about religious people in the last days. Second Timothy 3:5 says that one of the characteristics of people in the last days is they will have a form of godliness but will resist the power of it.

I don't want to be that way, and I don't want any of you to be that way. Let's not resist the power of God—let's welcome the power of God. We don't have to become weird; we don't have to become fruitcakes. What we do need to become is filled. You can call it whatever you want—a second work or a second grace or a baptism of the Holy Spirit. Call it whatever you want, but get it.

It was to this same church in Ephesus that Paul said in Ephesians 5:18: "Be filled with the Spirit." This isn't a one-time thing; it's not a two-time thing; it's not a five-time thing. It's a life-long thing. It's the posture, it's the position of our heart that says, "God if I'm going to serve You, I need power, I need grace, I need gifts. I can't do this on my own. I'm not going to trust slick speech. I'm not going to trust some great marketing campaign to win people to Christ."

I encourage you to get filled with the Holy Spirit and get bold in Him. Here's what you need to say: "I'm going to love Jesus first and foremost. I'm going to believe God that He's going to use me in spite of my frailties. I'm going to trust the Holy Spirit to fill me." That's what we need to return to. I can summarize all of this in one word: more. Because when you're in love, you want more.

4. They were magnifiers, worshipers of Jesus.

The Ephesian believers worshiped God. They received the Holy Spirit, God started doing signs and wonders in their midst, and the Holy Spirit came and glorified Jesus just like Jesus said He would. So, in that atmosphere of revival and great things happening, look at what it says happened in Ephesus:

> "This became known both to all Jews and Greeks dwelling in Ephesus; and fear fell on them all, and the name of the Lord Jesus was magnified"

> Acts 19:17

People in that community couldn't help but say, "Jesus, we love You. Jesus, we worship You. We're magnifying You. We're saying that You're bigger and better and more awesome than anything we've ever encountered here before. Oh, we know this is, you know, this is Ephesus and home to the temple of Diana, and we know this is the gateway into all of Asia. But none of it compares to You. And we're magnifying You and worshiping You."

Let's talk about true worship. Are you excited to sing the song of the Lord? Are you excited to come into church because you know when you come in it's an opportunity to enlarge your heart in His presence and make His praise glorious? Are you happy to come in because you know this is an opportunity to get with your Christian brothers and sisters and declare the greatness of God? Are you excited to magnify Jesus into the heavenlies? Are you willing to pray for an open heaven where God pours out His Spirit and people come to Christ? And are you ready to magnify Jesus for it? Is that what worship is like for you?

Or does it look like this? "(Yawn) Honey, we've sung that chorus thirty-seven times." Do you look around and see people who are miserable, or do you look around the room and see tears of joy and brokenness before God? Do you see people who are crazy in love with Jesus and say, "Wow, whatever he's doing, I want that! I want that close intimacy with Jesus"?

Does our worship bespeak first love? Or does it bespeak love grown cold? Jesus is challenging us to worship Him.

5. They were transparent before each other.

The Ephesians were transparent and humble with each other. They didn't care what people thought for a lick. Instead, what they cared about was what Jesus thought. They didn't care who was watching or what was going on—they were solely focused on Jesus and being about His business. Let me show you an interesting passage of scripture. Acts 19:18,19 says,

"And many who had believed came confessing and telling their deeds. Also, many of those who had practiced magic brought their books together and burned them in the sight of all. And they counted up the value of them, and it totaled fifty thousand pieces of silver."

Acts 19:18,19

The Ephesians were believers, but they were believers who still came to confess and tell of their ungodly deeds. They did it in front of many, and there were many who were doing it. They didn't say, "Oh gosh, what's my neighbor going to think if I go up to the altar and start crying and repenting and asking God to forgive me? What are they going to think, that I'm up here for doing some horrible thing—or something only kind of horrible?"

They didn't care! They were part of a community that said, "Hey, we're in this thing together with all of our baggage and all of our junk. We all need help. I'm at the top of the list. And so we're coming to a place that isn't just a hotel for the holy—it's a hospital for the hurting. And that's why I'm here because I haven't arrived, and I haven't gotten there yet, but I'm on my way. And I'm trying to get there through Christ, believing His promises and pressing into the truth."

They were all confessing, telling their deeds, and coming clean. They were magnifying and loving Jesus. They were receiving and getting filled with the Holy Spirit. They were being taught things they had never heard before. They were admitting, "I haven't heard of this before. I didn't know there was more, but I want it."

Let's go back to those five little things Jesus told them sixty years later through John in Revelation. To paraphrase, He said, "Hey, hey, return" because what started in revival was ending in rebuke. "Remember. Repent. Return. Come on. I love you too much not to tell you. Please come back. I miss you. I remember you. Will you remember me?"

Beloved, when that message was given to the church at Ephesus, I believe they had one of the most interesting altar calls ever. It wasn't an altar call for those who were sinfully wicked and stained with the stench of the world. It wasn't for people who were ignorant of the great Bible truths. It wasn't for people who had never shared their faith in Christ before. It was for people who were sound in doctrine, active in service, and moral in conduct. I believe there was an altar call in that little church in Ephesus that day, and I believe people who had never been to the altar since the time they came to Christ were at the altar saying, "Dear Jesus, forgive me. This surprised me. I never knew how far I had gotten away from You in the midst of doing so many things right." Maybe it was the pastor, the elders, the deacons. Maybe it was the people in the prayer ministry or the children's ministry. Or maybe it was the evangelists who had gotten so busy for Jesus that they had no time in Jesus.

So maybe right now God has spoken to your heart. Not Steve, God. He has spoken into your heart, and you've realized in the midst of your growth and maturity in certain things, Jesus is outside of it. You've realized that you need to return to your first love relationship, where your heart patters when it hears His name. Where you want to spend time with Him and talk to Him. You're ready to talk about Him to anybody who will listen. You're going to worship Him madly and passionately—and you don't care who is watching. You're here to give Him glory. God has spoken to your heart, and you're ready to say, "Jesus, I remember. Jesus, I repent. Jesus, I'm returning to the surprise and dismay of others in the body."

Church, I'm going to tell you the hope of this world is a church that is aflame with God's righteousness, power, and passion. That hope comes with spending quality time in the presence of the Lord Jesus Christ—that and that alone.

Let's get right with God in this way.

• • • • • • • • • • • • • • • • •

Lord, I didn't plan on this happening; I didn't know this was possible. I'm surprised that in the midst of Christian work and ministry and holy conduct and studying to show myself approved, that I've left You out, Lord. In the midst of preparing sermons or writing songs for others, I haven't been close to You. Jesus, I've contented myself with sound doctrine, active service, moral conduct. Jesus, I'm not here because I'm addicted. I'm not here because I'm living in some kind of rebellious, wicked sin. Jesus, I've left You behind. My prayer life shows that I'm not passionate about You. My worship life shows that I'm not passionate about You. God, I'm sorry this snuck up on me. Thank You for loving me and bringing me back. I remember. I repent. And I return.

Lord, without a bunch of hoopla and hype, we open our hearts and our hands. And we say, "Lord, please baptize me in the power of Your Holy Spirit—afresh, anew, maybe for the first time. God, would You empower me for the work that's in front of me? I can't do it without You. I know it's Your good pleasure to give the Holy Spirit to Your kids who ask. I receive Your power. More of You, Lord. More of You, Lord—because I love You, and I want more."

Lord, thank You for loving us enough to tell us the truth, to get us back into right relationship with You. And God, thank You that You want us in Your presence. That's unbelievable, Lord! Thank You for wanting us to draw near. Thanks, God. Thank You for bringing fresh life on Your sons and daughters. Lord, may this day be a new start in all of our lives, O God, at every level. May You increase in our hearts a love for the Lord Jesus Christ that we've never known before. We surrender to You, we love You, we worship You. Use our lives, Lord, for Your honor and glory. We love You, Lord. In Jesus' name, Amen, Amen, Amen, Amen, Amen.

Part 2

The church at Smyrna

2

PREFACE

*R*evelation 2:8–11 contains a sober message for all of us. I know it's only four verses, but in all seriousness, this is a weighty message. We are going to talk about suffering and what our response needs to be when we are suffering in and for Jesus. This isn't a lighthearted message. This isn't something where you are going, "Hallelujah, this chapter rocks!" Your experience with this text will be contemplative, it'll be soaking, and it will be, "Wow, I need to really think about some things, don't I?"

We are going to look at Jesus' message to the church of Smyrna. Before we really jump into it, I want to give you some background about the area of Smyrna so you can get a feel for what's going on in this passage.

Smyrna was about thirty-five miles north and up the coast from Ephesus (see Chapter 1). Smyrna rivaled Ephesus and Pergamus in its beauty. Smyrna was a very beautiful area because of its architecture and the streets. Smyrna had massive outdoor theaters that seated between twenty and fifty thousand people. They had elaborate Greek temples with all of their marbled glory. They had widely paved streets, which again was a testimony to their wealth and their affluence. Smyrna was a major harbor for shipping; it was a major business hub, and the society was wealthy. They also boasted to be the birthplace of Homer—not Simpson—Homer, you know, the other famous one you read about in the CliffsNotes in school. Smyrna was referred to (and this is important—I want you to remember this) as the "Crown of Asia" because of its beauty and its stature and its glory as a city.

Christians were under tremendous persecution in Smyrna. The Romans had issues with Christians, but in Smyrna, the Jews were more hostile to the Christians than the Romans. Interestingly enough, it's recorded in history that the Jews broke their own Sabbath law in Smyrna. They carried piles of wood on the Sabbath to create the bonfire that where Polycarp, the bishop of Smyrna, was martyred There was much hatred, persecution, martyrdom, and animosity from the Jews in Smyrna toward the Christians. Polycarp was the last personal disciple of John the Disciple (who wrote Revelation). He became the bishop of this church, and he was burned alive at the stake (and later died from a stab wound), not by the Romans but by Jews. So the religious atmosphere was pretty wild.

Smyrna was only one of two churches of the seven mentioned in Revelation where Jesus didn't have anything bad or corrective to say. He didn't have any rebuke for them; He had major comfort for them. Philadelphia was the other church that received no rebukes from Jesus, but we will get there in a few chapters.

The name Smyrna comes from the same root word as "myrrh"—you know, gold, frankincense, and . . . I'm making sure you are awake and that you didn't check out on me yet . . . myrrh. Here's the thing with it, myrrh only gets super fragrant when it is crushed. This is true of the church at Smyrna, and we'll see that it became fragrant the more it got crushed. It became the fragrance of Christ. Jesus had a word of hope and comfort for them, and dare I say, Jesus has a word of comfort for us in this passage. It's a message for those of us who may be feeling crushed and need to understand how to get through it.

• • • • • • • • • • • •

THE MESSAGE TO THE CHURCH AT SMYRNA

Listen to Jesus speaking in Revelation 2:8–11:

> "And to the angel of the church in Smyrna write, 'These things says the First and the Last, who was dead, and came to life: "I know your works, tribulation, and poverty (but you are rich); and I know the blasphemy of those who say they are Jews and are not, but are a synagogue of Satan. Do not fear any of those things which you are about to suffer. Indeed, the devil is about to throw some of you into prison, that you may be tested, and you will have tribulation ten days. Be faithful until death, and I will give you the crown of life. He who has an ear, let him hear what the Spirit says to the churches. He who overcomes shall not be hurt by the second death."
>
> Revelation 2:8–11

In this letter to Smyrna, Jesus gives us four lessons related to suffering that are incredibly applicable to us today:

1. You need to be eternally minded.

Jesus starts this letter by intentionally referring to Himself as someone who can help them. He is the First and the Last, the eternal God. Jesus says to this church that is being crushed and persecuted, "Hey, here's what you need to know about Me. You need to know that I was here before this trouble started, and I'm going to be here after it's over. I am the First and the Last. I am bigger than and outside of time and space, and I am looking into the affairs of men."

Jesus is very specifically trying to get the believers in Smyrna focused on His eternal majesty and His eternal authority.

He is trying to help them become "big picture people." It is imperative when we are going through a crushing tribulation that we are big picture and eternally minded people. If we're not looking with the sight of eternity at what God is doing in the Spirit, and if we are looking only at what is temporary and immediate and what is decaying, we will only see pain. When we only look at the pain, we become the most defeated. So Jesus says, "Hey Smyrna, crushed ones, here's what you need to know right away: I'm the First and the Last; I'm the eternal One; I'm bigger than anything you are going through. So get your sight right—you must do it. This world doesn't have the final word over your situation, but I do because I'm bigger than it, I'm outside of it, and yet present with you. **"Don't look at your pain; look at Me."**

Jesus also reminds them, "I was dead and came to life again." This was very important for their situation because they were facing death. They needed to know that even when they were dead in body, they would not really be dead. They needed to be reminded that in Christ, death doesn't have the final word over life. Death doesn't speak the final word, only Christ does, because Christ conquered death, hell, and the grave. Guess what? Death has no power over you or me. These believers were still going to be burned at the stake. They were still going to get their head chopped off, or whatever type of persecution they were facing. Whatever trial they were going through and whatever it was that might require their life, Jesus said, "Hey, even in death, don't despair—I'm in charge. **"Don't look at death; look at Me."**

Most of us are not facing immediate death, but when you are facing immediate death, guess where your focus needs to be—on eternal life. In His letter to Smyrna, Jesus repeats the exact words in Revelation 1:17, 18. Remember John's commentary on his encounter with Jesus?

"And when I saw Him, I fell at His feet as dead. But He laid His right hand on me, saying to me, 'Do not be afraid; I am the First and the Last. I am He who lives, and was dead, and behold, I am alive forevermore. Amen. And I have the keys of Hades and of Death.'"

Revelation 1:17, 18

Even Jesus said Amen to Himself—Amen! He also said, "I have the keys of Hades and of Death." He was reminding them of His eternal glory and victory over hell and death. When we're facing death, when we're facing persecution and tribulation, when we're facing a bad report from the doctor or a boss, when we're facing life-impacting situations, we need to allow the Holy Spirit to come behind us, gently grab us by the temples, point our eyes up to the King of Glory, and tell us, **"Don't look at the circumstances; look at Me."**

Jesus' words to Smyrna are also for our benefit and our blessing. Therefore, in the midst of our unbelievable pain and trial and tribulation and tragedy and devastation and destruction, we have to anchor our hope in Him and know it is going to be good. It might not feel good right now—we might be scared, we might be going through a tough time, we might be struggling to keep our spiritual life from drowning. What keeps us afloat in those desperate times is this: we know that He is going to work all things—all things that concern us, all things that are destroying us—He is going to work all things well according to the council of His own will. We don't need to be ashamed. We are not going to die, and then die, and then die. Ultimately whatever happens is going to be for our good and our blessing. We must keep looking at Him.

When bad things happen, if we keep looking at Him, we're strong. We're able to make it. It doesn't mean we're going to be perfect, it doesn't mean we're never going to break down or have a bad day. Those times are real. Ultimately, our soul and our spirit are anchored because we're looking at Him. His thoughts toward us are peaceful, not evil. His thoughts give us a future and a hope (*Jer. 29:11*), and even death doesn't have the final word over us as long as we keep looking at Him.

I couldn't help but think about how Job responded to his severe trials. You may remember the story and what happened to him. To summarize, Job was this totally righteous guy and the Enemy came along and told God, "Hey, let me get after him, and he will turn his back on you." God said, "Have at it; just don't kill him." So the Enemy went and did what? In one day Job got word that his wealth was gone and his children had been killed. In one day. Here's this guy who was totally righteous. I mean, if there was ever a time where life isn't fair. This was unjust and undeserved. Job must have thought, Lord, I've served You my whole life—what's going on?

Miraculously, Job wasn't the guy who confronted God and blamed God for what happened. Job 1:20–22 says,

> "Then Job arose, tore his robe, and shaved his head; and he fell to the ground and worshiped. And he said: 'Naked I came from my mother's womb, and naked shall I return there. The Lord gave, and the Lord has taken away; blessed be the name of the Lord.' In all this Job did not sin nor charge God with wrong."
>
> Job 1:20-22

Job was the guy who:

- Had his mind on eternity,
- Was a big picture person, and
- Chose to love and trust God no matter the circumstances.

When Job got this horrible word, he arose, tore his robe, shaved his head, fell to the ground, and worshiped. He worshiped? He ought to have been kicking and throwing dust and blaming God. No way. He worshiped. Why? Because he saw there was something bigger going on here than the loss of his wealth and his children. There was something more important, something more final than temporary death and pain. There was something bigger going on here, and he kept looking at God.

Job fell down and worshiped God. He said,

> "Naked I came from my mother's womb, and naked shall I return there. The Lord gave, and the Lord has taken away; blessed be the name of the Lord"
>
> Job 1:21

What was Job like? I am absolutely convinced that Job was a big picture guy who was spiritually minded. Even though he experienced the heartache and loss that was right in front of him, he knew there was a bigger picture. There was something more final than what he was experiencing here on Earth. He knew there was a greater authority behind the suffering and pain. He also knew that this greater authority was for him and not against him.

This is where we need to start pressing into the Word and saying to God, "You know what, Lord, let some of that Job stuff rub off on me. Do a work of grace in my heart, God, so that in the midst of being crushed by tribulation, I will praise You and worship You. I will not blame You. I will not get bitter with You. I'm going to magnify You and realize at the end of the day that You're for me. And even if my body dies, that's not the final word. Lord, You're for me, and what You have for me is way greater than anything that's going on right here." When you can say that, it is mature Christianity. It's something deeper than "Three Easy Steps on How to Have a Healthy Marriage."

I love the fact that God showed that He had the final word over Job's life and over the matter. In the end of the Book of Job, God blessed him more than he ever experienced. The Scripture says that Job ended up with fourteen thousand sheep, six thousand camels, a thousand yoke of oxen, a thousand female donkeys, seven sons, and three daughters who were more beautiful than any of the other girls in the land. In addition, Job lived another 140 more years, and he saw his offspring for four more generations. Then it says that Job died, old and full of days.

I am absolutely convinced that if Job would have wagged

his finger at God, blamed Him for how unfair this was, quit his faith, ran the other way, and said there is nothing to this God thing that his restoration would never have happened. Job is an example to all of us that we need to hang on and be eternally minded people. We can't just be around long enough to complain. We need to hang on long enough to be restored. We need to hang on long enough to be blessed. We need to hang on long enough to let God show us that He has the final word. It ain't over even when it's over; it ain't over even when the fat lady sings. It ain't over. God has the final word.

Now, whether God restores our lives this side of heaven or not, what He has for us in heaven is more than enough to comfort us and give us hope in the midst of today's tragedy. It is about being big picture people and spiritually minded enough that when our temporary world crumbles, we don't give up. Our hope and our joy and our peace isn't found in our American comfortable lifestyle—it's found in keeping ourselves eternally focused, with the big picture in mind and our eyes always looking at Him.

2. You need to know God as never before.

Revelation 2:9 says, "I know your works, tribulation, and poverty (but you are rich); and I know the blasphemy of those who say they are Jews and are not, but are a synagogue of Satan." Jesus says to the people in Smyrna, "I know your works. I know." I don't know if that does anything for you. I don't know if you've ever been in the pressure cooker, the blast furnace of suffering and persecution and trial and tribulation. I don't know if those words "I know" mean anything to you. They stood out to me, man, like that!

"I know."

"You do?"

"Yes, I know."

"Lord, You are intimately aware of every detail of my circumstance? You know? Lord, You mean I'm not forsaken, I'm not forgotten? You know? Lord, You mean this thing that's happening to me right now isn't something that slipped by You and then when You saw it You were surprised and panicked about how to fix it? God, You mean You know? Lord, You mean that whatever is going on in my life right now had to pass through the screen of Your permissive will? You're here? You're present? You're aware? You're grace? You're strength in my weakness? God, You know?"

Jesus says, "Hey, I know every detail of what you are going through."

Let me share something with you that isn't an easy pill to swallow. Beloved, there are some realities of God, some of His truths that are only known in the place of crushing suffering. There are some things that you will only know about God when He allows you to be crushed under the chariot wheel of your enemy.

Then, during that crushing, He says, "I know. I'm allowing this and I know. I am allowing you to experience this because you're not going to experience all of Me and more of Me unless you get to the depths of who I am. You see, Lazarus, I'm going to let you die so that people can know after the fact that I am the Resurrection and the Life."

Unfortunately we say, "No, no, no, no! We'll believe that You are the Resurrection and the Life, just don't prove it. We'll take You at Your word, but don't let Lazarus die."

Jesus says, "I know, I know, I really do know. I'm going to let this trial, this persecution, this sickness, this disease, this tragedy—exist for a while. I know. In the midst of it, you are going to understand Me in ways you never knew possible. You are going to see that in between breaths when you feel like your heart can't inhale one more time, I'm right there. I will give you the ability to take your next breath. When you have nothing because you've been devastated, and you can't imagine tomorrow, let alone the next second, I'm right there. I know."

Then, a year later, you realize, "I made it, didn't I? Wow. God, I made it. I didn't think I could. I remember when I was lying on the floor saying, 'Oh, God, I don't know if I can do one more day. I don't know if I can do this any more.' You said, 'Yes, you can. I'm going to give you what you need. Yes, you can.'" It's then that we realize He is more glorious than we ever knew before. God's Word is not just print on pages—it's reality in our hearts that can never be stolen.

Have you ever had the honor and the privilege of looking into somebody's eyes when they said something like this? "Man, this thing that happened to me rocked my world and shook me to the core. There were times and days of tremendous fear and frustration. Man, there were times when I didn't think I could take my next breath. But God got me through. I held on to Him, and He held on to me. I made it! I made it! As painful as it was and as scary as it was, I wouldn't trade it for anything! Because in the midst of this thing, I learned more about the grace and power and provision and preservation of God than I ever knew in all my other days combined."

That's going deeper; that's experiencing more of Him. That's knowing Him like never before.

Unfortunately, we don't really know much of God until God is all we have. Your spouse won't do, because he or she wasn't created to fulfill your every need—only Christ can. When your job won't do, when your bank account won't do, when the doctors won't do, when your medicine won't do, when nothing will do but God—if you ever have the unbelievable privilege of walking in that place, then you will know Him as you have never known Him before.

Paul understood the spiritual benefit of suffering in Christ. He didn't only understand it, he desired it. He asked for it. Philippians 3:10 says, "That I may know Him and the power of His resurrection, and the fellowship of His sufferings, being conformed to His death." What a great passage. "Oh, Lord, I want to know You and the power of Your resurrection." We are great at praying that part. "God, I want to know supernatural power. I want to see signs and wonders. I want to watch dead people come back to life and deaf people hear and blind people see. God, sign me up—I want to be Your man of the hour with Holy Ghost power."

When was the last time, like Paul, that you said, "Oh, God, please, please give me the unbelievable honor and privilege of entering into the fellowship of Your sufferings. Lord, help me to understand what it felt like to be rejected by family members—to have them think I'm crazy for loving You.

"Lord, help me to understand what it felt like to be in the Garden. What did it feel like to have friends, friends You needed and wanted to be close by, who You found sleeping during the biggest hour of crisis in Your life? God, help me to know and enter into the fellowship of that pain and suffering. Lord, allow me to feel what You felt when You hung there alone on the Cross and people mocked You. God, fashion my heart in such a way that I would know not only the fellowship of Your sufferings, but more importantly, the depth of the grace of our Father who allowed You to endure it all and to know Him in greater ways than ever before, through Your suffering."

We don't pray much like that, do we?

I'm all for the power of His resurrection, and I'm not going to stop praying for that. I'm wondering what it would be like if we as Christians matured to the point of the apostle Paul and were able to say, "Look, let me taste Your sufferings, because I know that Your suffering is the only thing that produces greater depth of character in me than I've ever known before."

C. S. Lewis said, "God whispers to us in our pleasures, speaks in our conscience, but shouts in our pains: it is His megaphone to rouse a deaf world."[1] Sometimes suffering is the only thing that will cause us to bow the knee, to cry out to Him, and to be desperate for Him. Suffering for Christ—what a privilege, what an honor! What a way to fully know Him as never before!

I know, we are used to praying for the poor people around this globe who are being persecuted and martyred as we speak right now—people who are huddled in underground catacombs in China. I know we pray for them because they've got it so rough. Beloved, do you know that they pray for us because we've got it so easy? Do you know they pour their hearts out because we have missed out on the deeper things of God because we've satisfied ourselves with the comfort of His blessing? I don't say that to make us feel bad. I just want to make sure we have our stuff and our stuff doesn't have us.

Some things we'll never know apart from suffering. And God is happy to allow us to enter into those circumstances so we might know Him as never before.

3. You need to not be afraid of suffering.

> "Do not fear any of those things which you are about to suffer. Indeed, the devil is about to throw some of you into prison, that you may be tested, and you will have tribulation ten days. Be faithful until death, and I will give you the crown of life."
>
> Revelation 2:10

Jesus said, "Because of who I am and what I offer you both in the midst of your suffering and after your suffering ceases, don't be afraid. Keep your eyes on Me. Be spiritually minded, be eternally minded, and keep your eyes on the big picture. I'm in charge, I'm in control. You might not like how this feels, but I'm working a far exceeding weight of glory in your life. Don't be afraid."

Have you ever wondered why Christians suffer? I believe there are four reasons why Christians suffer:

- ***Christians suffer because of ungodly behavior.***
  Sometimes we suffer because of the lifestyle that we choose to live. The church in Corinth was a church that was wrought with flesh and carnality and problems. When they came together, they partook of the Lord's Supper, the bread and the cup, in a very irreverent, flippant man-ner. They didn't discern how glorious, holy, sacred, and special it was to partake of Communion. So they'd eat some bread and drink some wine. They would eat it and drink it in this irreverent manner.
  Paul blasted them and said, "Hey, this is what you

need to know." First Corinthians 11:29–32 says, "For he who eats and drinks in an unworthy manner [or irreverent manner] eats and drinks judgment to himself, not discerning the Lord's body. For this reason many are weak and sick among you, and many sleep. For if we would judge ourselves, we would not be judged. But when we are judged, we are chastened by the Lord, that we may not be condemned with the world."

In other words, He is always working in us so that we are not ultimately condemned. Sometimes we suffer because of our ungodly behaior.

- *Christians suffer to prevent pride.*

This is interesting. You know the apostle Paul is one of the most unique people that ever walked the Earth. He experienced revelations, visions, dreams, encounters with God, God teaching him one-on-one. He was a fabulous preacher, teacher, and he had a great mind. He witnessed miraculous healings, He cured all kinds of stuff, He delivered people from demons. Paul was a powerhouse. He had every possibility of becoming prideful and arrogant because of "look at how God uses me!"

In 2 Corinthians 12:7 Paul wrote, "And lest I should be exalted above measure by the abundance of the revelations, a thorn in the flesh was given to me, a messenger of Satan to buffet me, lest I be exalted above measure." Sometimes, beloved, we suffer just to keep us humble.

- *Christians suffer to learn trusting obedience.*

Look at Hebrews 5:8 and what it says about Jesus: "Though He was a Son, yet He learned obedience by the things which He suffered." Jesus learned to trust the Father and to walk in trusting obedience even in the midst of His suffering.

- **Christians suffer as a testimony of Jesus' preserving grace and power.**

In Acts 9:16, Jesus spoke about Paul's conversion on the road to Damascus. Jesus said, "For I will show him how many things he must suffer for My name's sake." Sometimes Jesus allows us to suffer as a testimony of His grace and preserving power. Sometimes Jesus allows us to suffer so that other people from the church and from the world can look at our faithful response to our devastating circumstance, just like Job. Sometimes we suffer so that people can look and say, "Wow, look at that—that person should be devastated, and yet they are more alive than ever. How is that possible?" Then that suffering person says, "By the grace of the Lord Jesus Christ—and He will do the same thing for you." Suffering happens sometimes as a testimony to Jesus.

My personal opinion was that Smyrna was suffering to learn trusting obedience and to be a testimony to the preserving grace of Jesus in the midst of crushing tribulation. Their trials would speak for centuries and tell us that we can faithfully suffer for Christ and be strengthened.

Jesus said to Smyrna, "Don't be afraid about the things you are going to suffer. The devil is about to throw some of you into prison to test you. The devil is going to see if your faith is real. He's going to try to get you to renounce your love and trust and adoration and worship of God. He thinks that if he can just wreak enough havoc in your life that you will forsake your Savior. So he's coming and he's going to mess with you and he's going to throw you into prison to test you."

Beloved, have you figured out yet that there are going to be times in your life where your faith gets tested? Where God says, "All right, Satan, go ahead. Go ahead"? It's really true. It doesn't mean God doesn't love you. It means that in the midst of that suffering, you will experience a far exceeding weight of glory. It means you are going to be more conformed into the image of the Lord Jesus Christ.

I can't help but think of Peter's words in 1 Peter 1:6, 7: "In this you greatly rejoice, though now for a little while, if need be, you have been grieved by various trials, that the genuineness of your faith, being much more precious than gold that perishes, though it is tested by fire, may be found to praise, honor, and glory at the revelation of Jesus Christ."

Peter said, "The genuineness of your faith is going to be tested. Sometimes it is going to be by fire, and the purpose of it is to purify your faith so that when Jesus comes back, you will have a faith that is honorable, praiseworthy, and glorifying to His kingdom."

Years later, Peter's faith was tested. Church history tells us he was crucified upside down because he told his executioners, "I am not worthy to be crucified in the way that my Lord was." He passed the test. He endured the suffering. He lived his own sermon.

James, the half brother of Jesus, said, "My brethren, count it all joy when you fall into various trials, knowing that the testing of your faith produces patience" (*James 1:2, 3*). I know some of you are saying, "I'm patient enough. I've got all the patience I need. Lord, don't test my faith." The testing of your faith produces patience. It is working something in you so that you can learn to not be afraid.

Years later, James died a violent martyrs' death. His faith was tested big time. Yet he exercised patience, and he became mature and complete. He lacked nothing. He wasn't afraid, even at the very point of his death.

In Revelation 2:10, Jesus basically told the church of Smyrna, "The devil's going to throw you into prison; you are going to be there, and it's going to be for a certain amount of time. This testing is going to be for ten days." Commentators aren't sure whether it is a literal ten days or not. They don't know whether it was ten years under the Roman emperor Diocletian, who persecuted the church for ten years, or if it was the ten Roman emperors who would persecute the church until the time of Constantine.

The point is, nobody knows for certain, but it was for a predetermined time. What we have to understand is the fact that Jesus knew how long it would last. One more time, this tells me He is in charge. If I know that He's in charge, that He knows what is going on in my life, that I haven't been forgotten or forsaken, then I know I can make it. I can say, "I am not afraid . . . because of Him."

Jesus said, "Be faithful until death, and I will give you the crown of life" (*Rev. 2:10*). I love this. Jesus occasionally has a sense of humor—just every once and a while—and if you're not sharp, you'll miss it. Do you remember what I told you Smyrna was called? The "Crown of Asia." Jesus was poking fun at their depraved, worldly system. He was saying, "Hey, be faithful until death, and I'll give you more than the Crown of Asia. Greek marble temples? Big deal. You haven't seen Orion from my perspective at all. You're looking at your paved cobblestone streets? Wow, let Me show you streets that are paved with gold. Pal, you ain't seen nothing yet. You're fascinated with the Crown of Asia, but I will give you the elaborate, glorious crown of life, the victor's crown of life that comes from putting your faith and trust in Me and holding on until I come to get you."

By poking fun at their worldly system, Jesus helped the believers in Smyrna to be eternally minded in the midst of their temporary struggles.

4. You need to hear what the Spirit is saying.

"He who has an ear, let him hear what the Spirit says to the churches. He who overcomes shall not be hurt by the second death."   Revelation 2:11

Jesus said, "Let the churches (plural) hear." That applies

to us, even two thousand years later. Let us read what He's saying to us about this issue of suffering, tribulation, trials, and being crushed for Christ so that He can be formed in us. Let's listen to what He is saying.

Did you hear anything from the Spirit as you read this verse? I read this scripture and pushed back from my studies and just prayed, "Lord, as a believer, as one of Your sons before You right now, I've read and I've heard and I've studied. What is it that You're saying?" Instantly, Scripture and truths began to go off in my mind as fireworks. What's the Spirit saying to me? He's saying, **"Be an overcomer!"**

Romans 8:18 says,

> "For I consider that the sufferings of this present time are not worthy to be compared with the glory which shall be revealed in us."
>
> Romans 8:18

Paul's telling us that we're going to suffer. We're going to go through tough times. You know what? It doesn't compare one lick to what God has waiting for those of us who love Him and are called according to His purpose and who are going to enter into heaven's glory. It doesn't compare.

So how do we move from where we are to what God has waiting? We need to be eternally minded. We need to learn obedience. We need to give testimony, and we need to listen to what the Spirit is saying.

Let's look at what God said to Joshua: "Have I not commanded you? Be strong and of good courage; do not be afraid, nor be dismayed, for the Lord your God is with you wherever you go" (*Josh. 1:9*).

That's not just a statement limited to Joshua thousands of years ago. It's a spiritual application for us today. It says, "If you walk into a bad appointment with your boss; if you walk into a bad report from a doctor; if you have lost your house, lost your health, or lost your whatever, I am with you wherever you go. Don't be afraid, don't be dismayed, and hold on! Don't let go! Don't quit! Don't give up! Be an overcomer because I am with YOU!" That's what I hear the Spirit saying to me, and He's saying it to you, too.

Beloved, listen to me. We don't think of cowardice as sinful behavior. But do you know that cowardice is one of the defining characteristics of people who don't make it into heaven?

> "But the cowardly, unbelieving, abominable, murderers, sexually immoral, sorcerers, idolaters, and all liars shall have their part in the lake which burns with fire and brimstone, which is the second death."
>
> Revelation 21:8

This verse talks about those who are outside of heaven, and it says they are cowards—they weren't willing to pay the price or pray the price. They weren't willing to hold on when all things were tough. They were cowards and weaklings. They weren't set in their minds before the persecutions happened, so they weren't prepared to say, "I'm sticking with Jesus. I want to be an overcomer. With Your help, Lord, I'm ready."

Unfortunately they backed off and shied away and languished in mediocrity when somebody needed to be a giant and stand up and say, "I'm not quitting no matter what." Beloved, I pray for an outpouring of boldness in the body of Christ. I pray that cowardice would disappear.

We need to make a decision. Are we in this eternally minded, bold, listening to the Spirit, with overcoming faith for life through hell and high water and everything else? Or are we chameleon, fly-by-night, mamby-pamby Christians? Are you going to be a Christian as long as the music is nice and you like it and the seats are comfortable and the air conditioning is just right and the preacher doesn't go too long?

Would we love Jesus if somebody stuck a gun barrel to our head and said, "Deny Him or your brains are going to be wallpaper?" The time to decide isn't when the gun is pressed against our temple. The time to decide that is now. It's time to strengthen your Spirit, draw the line in the sand, and show your colors. Don't be a coward. Don't be weak. Be an overcomer, not overcome.

Let me share what else the Spirit is saying. Let's read John 16:33: "These things I have spoken to you, that in Me you may have peace. In the world you will have tribulation; but be of good cheer, I have overcome the world." He's saying, "In Me you can have peace. In the world there are going to be problems, but in Me you can have peace and be unafraid. I have overcome the world. I'm in you, and you're in Me." We are one spirit in Christ. We're in this mess together. Therefore, if He's an overcomer, we're overcomers. We can do all things and endure all things with His help.

> "You are of God, little children, and have overcome them, because He who is in you is greater than he who is in the world."
>
> 1 John 4:4

I can be an overcomer because of Christ in me. Make sense? Then let's start pursuing that reality. Let's say, "Enough of, 'Oh God, You love me when I'm unfaithful, so I'm going to run that treadmill of unfaithfulness, Your faithfulness, unfaithfulness, Your faithfulness.'" Why don't we start pressing into God and saying, "God, I'm going to be faithful. I'm going to be an overcomer because of Your greatness in me, not myself."

John wrote something else about this overcoming spirit in 1 John 5:4:

> "For whatever is born of God overcomes the world. And this is the victory that has overcome the world—our faith."
>
> 1 John 5:4

Have you been born of God? Then you have all you need to be an overcomer. In Revelation 12:11, it's John again who writes about overcoming:

"And they overcame him by the blood of the Lamb and by the word of their testimony, and they did not love their lives to the death."

Revelation 12:11

I don't want to be overcome by circumstance. I don't want to be so spiritually soft and out of shape that if something knocks me upside the head I'm out for the count. I want to be strong enough so that I can stand up and say, "Come on!" Don't you? That's why we love the Rocky movies—we all want to be him. Even you girls, you want to be Rock-ette—you want to go and overcome!

Let's be overcomers.
 Check out Jesus' final words to the church at Smyrna:

"Be faithful until death, and I will give you the crown of life"

Revelation. 2:10

The second death won't have any power over you. When death, hell, and the grave get thrown into the lake of fire, man, it doesn't have anything to do with you. The second death has no power over you. The judgment of God, the wrath of God being poured out on cowards, unbelievers, and sexually immoral people doesn't have anything to do with us. Hallelujah to God!
 Beloved, in the midst of suffering and crushing trial and tribulation, let's determine right now that we're going to be faithful no matter what comes our way. Let's be overcomers in and by the power of the resurrected Christ whose grace is sufficient for all of us in everything.

And the church said, "Amen"—may it be so.

• • • • • • • • • • • • • • • • • •

Part 3

The churches at Pergamos and Thyatira

3

PREFACE

$\mathcal{B}$e prepared—we are getting ready to go where few dare to tread. Let's face it—people, and especially pastors, want to avoid controversy. Many pastors are afraid that people will misunderstand them and leave their churches. They are afraid the people will take their money and go home. Consequently, they pander to the people in the pew. They refuse to tread into the tough subjects. They say "fluffy" things that they assume the people want to hear, and they stay away from controversial topics. I'm not going to do that in this chapter. We're going to learn from the truth of the Bible.

Before we begin, I want you to know that these are not the words of an angry, self-righteous, condemning, fill-in-the-blanks, stereotypical, right-winged, politically correct fundamentalist. This is the truth of the gospel. This is the truth of the Word of God that is spoken with a huge amount of love. I believe the very fact that I am writing and speaking on this topic is a loving act, and I'm lovingly going to teach this important message.

What's not loving, beloved, is to know someone who is sick, to have the cure, and to do nothing about it because you're afraid you might offend the person by pointing out his or her illness. It's not loving to be silent—ever. It's not loving to know the cure and hide it—ever. It's also not loving to be a jerk when you speak or write. It's not loving to be arrogant. It's not loving to be condescending.

Essentially, we have two opposite ends of the spectrum in which the church operates. Either we say, "Well, I'm loving you by not saying anything that will rattle your cage or contradict your lifestyle" or we say, "We're over here totally contradicting people's lifestyles with hatred on our faces and in our veins." The sad thing about this is that both sides of this spectrum cause the truth to be unheard. When you are yelling and screaming and being self-righteous and arrogant toward people, they aren't going to hear a word you say. On the other hand, if you don't say anything, you'll be guaranteed the same result—they aren't going to hear a word you say. It's like fishing. There's a 100 percent chance that you aren't going to catch a fish if you leave the bait in the boat. You might catch your foot with the hook, but that's not why you went fishing.

We have to balance this spectrum as if on a tightrope when it comes to all biblical truth and reality. We need to share God's Word in love. We are going to walk this tightrope of truth and love. We aren't going to err or fall off on one side or the other. We aren't going to be mean-spirited, self-righteous people, although there are whole sections of the church that would love and applaud that. We're not going to be the silent, non-confrontational people, although there are whole sections who would love that, too. We're going to walk the tightrope of truth and love, and we're going to do it with a godly attitude and loving heart.

Here's another fact—when you speak the truth in love, your companions are going to be few. Most of the time you are going to get hit from both sides of the spectrum. You're going to get hit from the people who say you're not being loving, and you're going to get hit by those who say you should just be condemning. Therefore, what you and I have to do as Christians who speak the truth in love is be willing to be hated for our adherence to the truth just as the apostle Paul was (Paul writes in Galatians 4:16, "Have I therefore become your enemy because I tell you the truth?").

Are you willing? Because if you aren't willing to be hated for speaking the truth from God's Word, then your Christianity is not going to go very far, and it's not going to be very deep. Your Christianity is only going to last until someone gets tired of hearing what you have to say, and then you're going to fold it in and pander to them. You'll come to a point where you'll care more about them than you do about God and His Word. It's a delicate balance. It's a very hard job, and you could lose some friends.

I'm sad that many Christians, when confronted with truth, leave the church. It seems that there are people in churches today who pass every bit of Christian teaching through some higher filter in their mind. They say, "I'll allow Christian truth to come through this higher filter that I have, but if Christian truth ever contradicts this higher filter that I have in my life, then it's out and I'm out." The filters are all kinds of different things. There are political filters—extreme right, extreme left, or whatever in the middle. There are political filters that say, "I'll be a Christian so long as it doesn't affect or challenge what I believe politically." Then when they hear something that challenges the filter, they immediately bail on the whole Jesus thing. That's what breaks my heart and what makes me sad. When people do that, they are placing something—the idol of politics, the idol of political correctness, the idol of personal will, the idol of ego, or whatever idol it may be—above and beyond God's very Word.

That's what's sad to me, and it breaks my heart. Filtering truth through anything other than God's Word means you're not willing to let God be God in your life. You're not willing to let His Word be the only true filter of how you view the world. When you use these other filters, you don't have a biblical worldview— you've got a political worldview or a cultural worldview or some other kind of worldview besides a biblical worldview. I get it if you're a lost pagan. Have at it. What's heartbreaking is people who name the name of Christ who have these filters other than God's Word. I've seen it for years, and I've heard it for years. I've read their e-mails for years, and it's heartbreaking.

● ● ● ● ● ● ● ● ● ● ● ● ● ● ● ● ●

THE MESSAGE TO THE CHURCHES: TWO LETTERS

We are going to look at the church in Pergamos and the church in Thyatira because Jesus issued the same two overriding themes of correction to both of them. But before we begin, a couple of things are imperative. First, this lesson is hard, and I don't want you to check out. Don't just skim these pages and hope to quickly move to the next chapter or lesson. Stay focused, as there's a lot to learn. Second, it's critical that you know from the beginning that this is not about hatred, discrimination, condemnation, prejudice, or some form of phobia. In fact, it's an act of love to speak the truth in love out of concern for people's souls.

This chapter is about speaking biblical truth with clarity and conviction and without apology. The issues we'll explore are getting increasingly cloudy, not just out in the world, but also in the church itself. The central question is this: will we allow our lives to be ruled by the truth of the Word of God or will we go with the opinions of men that are craftily marketed, deceitful lies? Where do we stand on this issue?

I'm getting increasingly concerned about our children and the way they are being shaped and formed by the attitudes of the world. Being from California, I pay a lot of attention to what is going on in California. I was saddened to hear that it was the eighteen- to thirty-year-olds who were really the driving force trying to undo Proposition Eight, which states that marriage is between one man and one woman. It is the thirty and under group that have a mindset that says, "No, this is right—this proposition doesn't need to be there for anybody, and it's okay to have other definitions of marriage." I've got to tell you young folks—that's wrong. That's radically wrong. I hope and pray that as you read the Word of God, you'll develop a biblical worldview and a biblical perspective on all issues, including marriage. I'm not saying you should become mean and self-righteous, but I am saying that you need to understand the Word of God and take a stand for it today and everyday, because the world isn't getting any better.

This chapter is about understanding Jesus' heart. He wants all people to acknowledge their sin when it's presented to them and repent, turning to Him for forgiveness and cleansing instead of whitewashing what they do and calling their evil good. Jesus has a message of correction for the churches of Pergamos and Thyatira. It's a message about devilish compromise and sexual immorality in the church, as well as in the world. Jesus is about to get serious! Jesus is about to rattle every single one of us. Here's the entire letter to Pergamos in Revelation 2:12–17:

> "And to the angel of the church in Pergamos write, 'These things says He who has the sharp two-edged sword: "I know your works, and where you dwell, where Satan's throne is. And you hold fast to My name, and did not deny My faith even in the days in which Antipas was My faithful martyr, who was killed among you, where Satan dwells. But I have a few things against you, because you have there those who hold the doctrine of Balaam, who taught Balak to put a stumbling block before the children of Israel, to eat things sacrificed to idols, and to commit sexual immorality. Thus you also have those who hold the doctrine of the Nicolaitans, which thing I hate. Repent, or else I will come to you quickly and will fight against them with the sword of My mouth. He who has an ear, let him hear what the Spirit says to the churches. To him who overcomes I will give some of the hidden manna to eat. And I will give him a white stone, and on the stone a new name written which no one knows except him who receives it.'"
>
> Revelation 2:12–17

Here's the letter to Thyatira in Revelation 2:18–29:

> "And to the angel of the church in Thyatira write, 'These things says the Son of God, who has eyes like a flame of fire, and

His feet like fine brass: "I know your works, love, service, faith, and your patience; and as for your works, the last are more than the first. Nevertheless I have a few things against you, because you allow that woman Jezebel, who calls herself a prophetess, to teach and seduce My servants to commit sexual immorality and eat things sacrificed to idols. And I gave her time to repent of her sexual immorality, and she did not repent. Indeed I will cast her into a sickbed, and those who commit adultery with her into great tribulation, unless they repent of their deeds. I will kill her children with death, and all the churches shall know that I am He who searches the minds and hearts. And I will give to each one of you according to your works. Now to you I say, and to the rest in Thyatira, as many as do not have this doctrine, who have not known the depths of Satan, as they say, I will put on you no other burden. But hold fast what you have till I come. And he who overcomes, and keeps My works until the end, to him I will give power over the nations—'He shall rule them with a rod of iron; they shall be dashed to pieces like the potter's vessels'—as I also have received from My Father; and I will give him the morning star. He who has an ear, let him hear what the Spirit says to the churches.'"

Revelation 2:18–29

There are three phrases in these two passages that appear only in the Book of Revelation. Jesus told the church at Pergamos: "Satan's throne is there" and "Satan dwells there." Then to the church at Thyatira He said, "You are practicing the depths of Satan." The throne of Satan, the dwelling place of Satan, and the depths of Satan. Isn't it interesting that the only place those phrases are mentioned in Scripture is where this connection of sexual immorality and devilish compromise are mentioned together? This gets my attention, and it lets me know what's behind it very clearly.

DEVILISH COMPROMISE

Why is this issue of devilish compromise such a big deal? Let's look at an example of compromise in 1 Corinthians 10:18–22—eating things sacrificed to idols:

Observe Israel after the flesh: Are not those who eat of the sacrifices partakers of the altar? What am I saying then? That an idol is anything, or what is offered to idols is anything? Rather, that the things which the Gentiles sacrifice they sacrifice to demons and not to God, and I do not want you to have fellowship with demons. You cannot drink the cup of the Lord and the cup of demons; you cannot partake of the Lord's table and of the table of demons. Or do we provoke the Lord to jealousy? Are we stronger than He?

1 Corinthians 10:18–22

Jesus brought this indictment against the Corinthian church through the apostle Paul's pen thirty years before the Book of Revelation was written. He said, "I don't want you to eat meat sacrificed to demons because when you do, you are opening yourself up to fellowship with demons. I don't want you to fellowship with demons."

Right now you are probably saying, "Hey, Steve, I really don't have a problem with eating meat sacrificed to demons; I buy my meat at Kroger." Here is the issue: the Corinthians were to avoid meat sacrificed to idols because there was demonic power associated with it. It's a clear position. We, too, need to stay away from anything that has demonic power associated with it.

The issue then was that these teachers who were teaching the doctrine of Balaam were saying it was okay in the church. They said, "We know you are hungry, so go ahead and eat the meat. Jesus understands. He understands that the store was closed and you had to eat this. Go ahead and do it; it's okay to compromise."

But Jesus said, "You've been compromising, and I have it against you." It's not a light issue. In the midst of their idolatrous compromise, in the midst of allowing something else to have a place in their heart besides God, they were opening themselves up to strongholds and footholds of Satan himself. We need to be careful what we enthrone in our hearts. Why? Because fellowship with demons is very possible. This is not my opinion—it's what's in the Bible.

What we have to seriously watch is the compromise that comes to us today, even in the midst of some churches, that tells us that Jesus is all right with us sacrificing to our own devilish modern-day idols. Believe His Word—He isn't all right with it.

I'm talking about the idol of sexual immorality and its constant beckoning of people to sacrifice and worship at its lust-filled demonic altar that's at the center of the problem. It's the lie that if we just worship it and sacrifice to promiscuity and sexual immorality then we'll really be free. It's the lie that compels us to not put ourselves under the commandments, the laws and the rules of God. It's the lie that says, "Break Free! Live Free!"

Tell me, will we be free to get AIDS? If we "break free" to be promiscuous, can we still have sexually transmitted diseases? Is there freedom in that? Have any of you been by the bedside of someone dying of AIDS because they lived sexually immoral lives? It's depressing, devastating, and filled with loss and regret and "I wish I wouldn't have."

This "freedom" comes so well packaged. They say, "Come on, it's all right. Do what makes you feel good." It's all over television. It's everywhere. You can't buy a package of hot dog buns without some hunk or some hottie suggestively dressed. What's that got to do with hot dog buns? What's that got to do with the car I buy? We're bombarded with an unending onslaught of sexual perversion and promiscuity. Sexual immorality is everywhere.

Sexual immorality finds its way into the church, and it finds its way into the pulpits. Sadly, what comes out of the pulpit after sexual immorality makes its way into the church is heresy and ungodly—two things that Jesus hates, things over which Jesus spoke radical judgement. And yet we have churches in America and around the world promoting the gospel of sexual immorality. I want to be clear here in case I haven't been. It is the sin of sexual immorality. It's not the choice of sexual immorality, and it's not the lifestyle of sexual immorality. It's the sin of sexual immorality. It's wrong. Before anyone gets too worked up, let me tell you specifically to whom I'm writing.

I'm not just talking to homosexuals. I'm not just talking to heterosexuals. I'm not just talking to people who do immoral things outside of marriage. I'm also not just talking to people inside of marriage who still use pornography and are foul before God. I'm not just talking to one group—I'm talking to anyone who is committing the sin of sexual immorality.

My dad came up to me one day and said, "I'll tell you one thing, Son—you keep preaching like that, and you'll be preaching to a handful in your living room." I said, "I'm okay with that!" That would be fine with me. I've done it before, and I can do it again if it means that I'm preaching the Word of God without compromise.

This chapter is for everybody. This isn't the pastor just beating up on men and letting women off the hook. This is for all of us to look at our lives with the backdrop of Scripture and to ask ourselves, "Where am I in this deal, and who am I? What is Jesus saying to me?" The sin of sexual immorality is the same age-old, devilish doctrines of Balaam and Jezebel that are being heralded from pulpits across the land.

I want to give you a brief tour of the Scriptures, both Old Covenant and New, to see four things God says about any sexual relations outside of marriage between a man and a woman—because sexual immorality includes heterosexual fornicators and also pornographers, not just homosexuals. It's all sin, and we need to say what it is.

1. It's an abomination.

Leviticus 18:22 says, "You shall not lie with a male as with a woman. It is an abomination."

It just doesn't get any clearer that this. Homosexuality is an abomination and a stench in God's nostrils! Homosexuality has never been initiated, endorsed, or blessed by God anywhere in the Bible. It's not found in Scripture because it is unnatural—it can't multiply, bear fruit, or leave a legacy. It is always wrong, and it always brings God's judgment! Always.

I remember sixteen years ago when my wife and I spent a weekend in Palm Springs. We went over to the newspaper stand, and on the front of USA Today, there was an article written about how they had proven that people are born homosexual. I read it, and the article's writers had no proof at all. They hope to find a gene that proves homosexuality is not a choice. Therefore, their logic goes on to say, if it's not a choice, it's something I'm not accountable for, and I can live anyway I want.

Let me set the record straight. We're not born this way. We're not born sexually immoral, and we're not born fornicators. It's a result of not wanting to retain God in our knowledge and thereby giving ourselves over to ungodliness. More ungodliness leads to more ungodliness. Soon, we are doing those things that are sinful and shameful in the eyes of God.

2. It leads to death.

Read Romans 1:26–28:

> For this reason God gave them up to vile passions. For even their women exchanged the natural use for what is against nature. Likewise also the men, leaving the natural use of the woman, burned in their lust for one another, men with men committing what is shameful, and receiving in themselves the penalty of their error which was due. And even as they did not like to retain God in their knowledge, God gave them over to a debased mind, to do those things which are not fitting.
>
> Romans 1:26–28

What does the Scripture say very clearly? That this kind of behavior is shameful. Paul, the writer of Romans, goes on to say that these people actually received in themselves the penalty that was due them. They received the penalty of their error.

Nearly twenty-five years ago, when AIDS was a hot topic, I was a new Christian. I remember many Bible commentators asking if the HIV/AIDS epidemic was God's judgement on people who had been immoral. I don't know the answer, but it's interesting. It's something to think about.

Romans 1:32 says that people who practice sexually immoral lifestyles are worthy of death. That doesn't mean we start killing people. It doesn't mean we become arrogant, mean-spirited, and stupid. In the name of Jesus, please don't do that. However, remember that this kind of unrepentant lifestyle is worthy of death and eternal separation from God. There's nothing right about it.

Romans 1:32 goes on to say that it is not just those who practice sexual immorality who are deserving of death, but also those who approve of others doing it. Does that wake anybody up in here? There are whole strains that run through the church saying, "That's not for me, but I don't want to begrudge anyone else from doing it. If someone wants to do it, have at it." It's not just a passive issue with the homosexual community, and it's not just saying we want civil unions. It's infringing on holy, God-ordained marriage between a man and a woman. For the first time in American history (this is a biblical statement, not a political statement), the president-elect stood up and guaranteed gay rights in his acceptance speech. What's the deal? That's giving approval of those who do this, and Paul's letter is very clear that approval leads to death as well.

Politicians are saying, "This is all right, we're not going to discriminate." Friends, nobody's talking about discriminating, but how about not promoting? Why is someone's sexual orientation what someone needs to be known for? I don't go around talking about my sex life with my wife. Why is orientation the identity in this group? Why is it that people feel the unbelievable need today to condone it, support it, and approve of it when the apostle Paul says that if you approve of it, you're in the wrong camp? That's Bible, not Berger. It's not Republican, it's not right wing, it's not left wing—that's Bible, and that's Christian.

It's not just our federal leadership, either. The mayor of Los Angeles got up and told everybody at an anti-Proposition Eight rally, "The Jesus I love and the Jesus I pray to wasn't just about being a shepherd, He was about bringing everybody in. Let's not discriminate."

Doesn't that sound nice? The problem is, he's putting Jesus' stamp of approval on sexually immoral behavior that Jesus Himself says is wrong. This kind of public affirmation affects people in the church, and it affects Christians who really do love Jesus but are ignorant about the teaching of Scripture. It was the prophet who said, "My people are destroyed for lack of knowledge" (Hos. 4:6). I'm pleading with you to educate yourself. I'm asking that you forget your politics and educate yourself on what the Scriptures say and then, once you have the knowledge, take a stand for it. Not in anger, but in passion, obedience, and biblical truth.

3. It leads to a loss of inheritance.

Let's examine 1 Corinthians 6:9–11:

Do you not know that the unrighteous will not inherit the kingdom of God? Do not be deceived. Neither fornicators, nor idolaters, nor adulterers, nor homosexuals, nor sodomites, nor thieves, nor covetous, nor drunkards, nor revilers, nor extortioners will inherit the kingdom of God. And such were some of you. But you were washed, but you were sanctified, but you were justified in the name of the Lord Jesus and by the Spirit of our God.

1 Corinthians 6:9–11

You need to make sure you aren't deceived. Unrighteous people aren't going to inherit the kingdom of God. In this scripture, the apostle Paul goes through and lists sexually immoral, sexually broken practices, and he says "Hey, man, there's hope because some of you used to be like this, and now you've changed through your encounter with the Lord Jesus." People, Jesus is the answer. Jesus isn't just the answer for heterosexual, pornography-addicted whatever. He's the answer for the sodomite. He's the answer for the homosexual. He's the answer for everybody.

The interesting thing about this whole issue is that the people who are in this sin seem to be the only group who refuses to admit that their sin is actually sin. I am an old drug addict, a fornicating loser. I admit that. I was wrong. You talk to thieves and drunkards, and they will tell you with a stolen bottle of beer in their hands, "This is wrong—nothing is right about this." But—and I don't know what it is about this particular area of sin—but people just don't see it the same way. Maybe it's such a stronghold because it's where Satan dwells and where his throne is and it's deeply entrenched. Maybe it's such a stronghold that people are given to sexually immoral lives, and they angrily refuse to admit that it is wrong.

The sad thing is that churches and politicians affirm sexually immoral people by telling them their compromise isn't sin and that it's okay. They tell them that Jesus is all right with it, and the problem with that is that it is obvious from Scripture that He is not all right with it. The problem is that people don't understand it can lead to a loss of a precious inheritance.

4. It leads to judgement and tribulation.

Let's look again at Revelation 2:22:

"Indeed I will cast her [Jezebel] into a sickbed, and those who commit adultery with her into great tribulation, unless they repent of their deeds."

Revelation 2:22

Jesus said He would cast Jezebel into a sickbed. Isn't that phrase interesting when we consider the life-hindering and life-taking diseases that accompany sexually immoral lifestyles? Is this sickbed the sexually transmitted diseases? Is it HIV/AIDS? It's something to consider.

It is amazing to read the medical studies done by both sides of this issue—by people who are pro-immoral lifestyles and anti-immoral lifestyles. Both sides have come to the conclusion that sexually immoral lifestyles, if not stopped, shave a minimum of eight and as much as twenty years from a person's life. People who have a sexually immoral lifestyle have a shortened life span.[1] In the New King James version, 1 Corinthians 6:9 uses the word "sodomite." It refers to the destroyers of human bodies. I don't want to be graphic, but if you read or hear about what's going on around us, you will see why the life spans of those who engage in immoral lifestyles are shortened. Clearly, it destroys and tears down a person's body. It's simply a case of people doing things that weren't created to be used the way they are being used.

Jesus said, "I'm going to throw this woman Jezebel into a sickbed." In the same verse, Jesus said He would bring great tribulation upon those who don't repent. Is that great tribulation casting them into a sickbed, or is it something else? I don't know. But I think we have to agree that when we know of the tribulation that eternal God is able to create, it's not a desirable thing to fall into. No doubt here—Jesus is serious about this issue.

In Revelation 2:23, Jesus said that He would kill Jezebel's children with death. Does it mean her children, or does it mean the children who follow her doctrine? I don't want to be one of her children, do you? It doesn't sound like what any of us are really looking for in life.

Jesus talked directly to these two churches in Revelation, Pergamos and Thyatira, and He's talking to us, too. He used some pretty scary words to get the attention of churches riddled with compromise, idolatry, and sexual immorality. But there are two things we can do right now to make changes.

DECIDE TO CHANGE

1. We must flee.

Read 1 Corinthians 6:13,18:

"Foods for the stomach and the stomach for foods, but God will destroy both it and them. Now the body is not for sexual immorality but for the Lord, and the Lord for the body. Flee sexual immorality. Every sin that a man does is outside the body, but he who commits sexual immorality sins against his own body."

1 Corinthians 6:13, 18

Paul again writes that we must flee sin and not compromise. It is sin and we should run from it. We need to get as far away as possible from it. All forms of sexual immorality are wrong, and we must get away from them.

Remember the story of Joseph and Potiphar's wife? He was working hard for the high-ranking Egyptian official, and the official's wife tried to lure him into her bed. Clearly she wanted an immoral lifestyle. However, what did Joseph do? HE RAN!! He fled. Later she turned on him and he wound up in prison, but God used him even in that prison. Joseph made the right choice and emerged as second in command in Egypt. He was trusted, and I have to think that some of that trust came to him because he chose to flee sexual immorality.

2. We must take it seriously.

Let's look at Revelation 21:8:

"But the cowardly, unbelieving, abominable, murderers, sexually immoral, sorcerers, idolaters, and all liars shall have their part in the lake which burns with fire and brimstone, which is the second death."

Revelation 21:8

Beloved, these are just a few passages from the Scriptures, and I don't know how it could be any clearer. I don't know how much more clearly God could show how serious He is about these issues of devilish compromise and sexual immorality. People inside and outside the church deny its sinfulness and deny the coming judgment and try to convince the rest of us that it is okay, but it's clearly not okay from a biblical perspective.

The Archbishop of Canterbury, Rowan Williams, in a lecture that was first delivered to members of the Lesbian and Gay Christian Movement called these scriptures that I just mentioned and scriptures like them "an abstract fundamentalist deployment of very ambiguous Biblical text".[2] He says scriptures that are very clearly against the pro-sexually immoral lifestyle that he promotes and endorses as the Archbishop of Canterbury are ambiguous.

When I read those biblical texts, I don't know how they could be any more unambiguous! How could they be more clear? The Archbishop reads and speaks eight different languages. I think he should practice his English some more and find out what these verses mean. This is troubling. This is a man who is responsible for the spiritual lives of millions of people, as he oversees the Anglican and Episcopal communion. In my opinion, he's a heretic and a blasphemer. He is ushering himself and others into the lake of fire faster than he realizes!

Unfortunately, the breakdown in morality isn't a small thing, but rather it's growing. This needs to be something that doesn't just make us mad, it needs to break our hearts. Read this list of Christ-confessing churches that approve sexually immoral behavior: Episcopal Church USA, Evangelical Lutheran Church, some United Methodist churches, Presbyterian Church USA, United Church of Christ Congregational, some Christian Church Disciples of Christ, and Metropolitan Church, just to name a few.

These churches are either full-blown in their promotion and approval of sexually immoral behavior or there are battles at the highest levels between leadership who wants to condone this kind of lifestyle and the local churches who confess Christ as Lord and believe His Word.

Personally, I quake when I think of the judgment that is coming their way if they don't repent. I quake when I think of the judgment coming our way for people in this room who refuse to repent of sexual immorality. There are heterosexual men and women committing fornication, men and women given to pornography, masturbation, and chronic wickedness. I quake to think that you think it's all right with God because society, politicians, and preachers have told you that it is. This pulpit will not be silent.

In Revelation 2:16, Jesus said He would fight against the sexually immoral churches with the sword of His mouth. He said He would fight against and judge them with His very Word. The is the very same Word the false teachers twist and pervert in order to get people to devilishly compromise and commit sexual immorality. I have a word of caution to anyone who chooses to twist and distort Jesus' words—don't pick a fight with the Ruler of this universe because you will lose.

THERE IS HOPE

- ### *Jesus Offers Repentance*
Now, let's get some hope in the air. There is always hope when Jesus is involved. Even in the midst of Jesus saying, "Hey man, it is this bad, it is this wrong, it is an abomination, it is a stench, and here's all of the judgment that surrounds it. Hello, people! This is obviously a very serious issue with Me on the highest level"—even in the midst of that, there is hope.

In both the letter to Pergamos and the letter to Thyatira, Jesus mentions repentance. He basically says, "Listen, there is still hope, because I am offering you the opportunity to repent." It never ceases to blow my mind how good Jesus is, how kind He is, how patient He is, and how loving He is. It never ceases to blow my mind to watch Him love people and invite them into relationship with Himself even when they've done the most heinous thing.

That's exactly the kind of hope He offers here. Part of the problem with people who have lived a life bound by sexual immorality is that they don't believe there is any hope. They don't believe they can change. They don't believe God would love them because some church treated them horribly and they don't think there's any hope for them. We have to say this: there's hope for everybody. And Jesus says, "Will you repent? Will you change directions? Will you let Me clean you up? Will you let Me change your life? Will you let Me sanctify you? Will you let Me wash you and make you clean? I want you to come back to Me, you can change, and there is hope." That's the hope He offered both churches—multiple times. Repent.

- ### *Jesus Offers Eternal Satisfaction*
I love this. Revelation 2:17 says, "To him who overcomes I will give some of the hidden manna to eat." Hidden manna? I love His word play. Jesus is saying, "Hey, you guys are all excited about eating things that were sacrificed to idols? How about eating something that I have? Hidden manna—the Bread of Life—that is eternally satisfying. You're hungry for something, and you keep looking for more and more. You get more and more, and you are more and more empty. The hope I offer you is to come and eat the Bread of Life. Come and eat the hidden manna I have for those who will seek Me. You will be eternally satisfied, and you will never hunger again." That's hope.

- ### *Jesus Offers a Pardon*
In Revelation 2:17, Jesus also offers a white stone to those who overcome and receive the hidden manna. Jesus says, "You guys are big on stones and idols that you chip away out of rocks. I've got a stone for you, and it's a white stone." In those days, when you were on trial you either got a white stone or a black stone. If you got a white stone, it was a declaration of your

innocence, your pardon, and your freedom. You had nothing held against you any longer. Nobody could touch you; you were free. Jesus said, "With your fascination with stone idols, take this white stone of pardon from Me, and you will really know what true freedom is all about."

- ### *Jesus Offers Real Intimacy*

Jesus offers repentance, satisfaction, pardon, and then, of course, He offers intimacy. Revelation 2:17 continues: "And on the stone a new name written which no one knows except him who receives it." Jesus says, "You know the white stone? Here's the deal: it's going to have a name written on it; it's going to be inscribed. And when someone else looks at it, they aren't going to understand what it says. It's a name that only you are going to know." I don't know what you think about Jesus, but I read stuff like that, and it melts my heart. Obviously He knows what it says, because He wrote it on there. He's God and He knows everything. He's saying, "I want to give you a white stone of pardon, and it's going to have our name that I call you inscribed on it. It's going to have My little pet name for you on it." That's real intimacy!

In the midst of a world that is literally dying for intimacy right now, Jesus says, "You're looking for intimacy? How about with the Son of God? How about with the Creator of the universe? How about letting Me be your everything?" The last bit of hope is just that—Jesus Himself.

- ### *Jesus Offers Himself*

Jesus moves past personal intimacy by offering Himself. In Revelation 2:28 He essentially says, "I'll give you the morning star! I'll give you Myself." God can't give any more than who He is because He is everything. He tells us, "I'll hold nothing back."

Friends, we are looking for love in all the wrong places. Whether you are heterosexual or homosexual, chances are you are trying to find satisfaction, fulfillment, and healing from things that happened to you when you were a kid. You are looking in all the wrong places. Men and women addicted to pornography who are trying to spice up your marriage, it's destroying your marriage. I had a lovely young woman come up to me after first service, sobbing and telling me that her husband is addicted to pornography and it's destroying their marriage. I'm just telling you what we deal with all the time. There are problems. Hear me: sexual immorality on all levels is sin and it's destructive. Jesus is serious about it, and He says, "Knock it off! Let Me be your satisfaction; let Me give you what you truly need."

High school students, I know that it is vogue and fashionable and cool to pretend to be gay or to say that you are bisexual. What has happened? I beg you, stop it! Stop it because you are playing with demonic strongholds and giving Satan access that you will regret for the rest of your life. You want intimacy? Find intimacy with Christ. It is pure, it is holy, it doesn't hurt, and it doesn't cause problems. It will build you up and give you an identity that you will love the rest of your life. Virgins, listen to me, in one second you can give away your virginity and become just like every other kid out there in society. But in their entire life, every other kid can never again become what you are right now. Don't give yourself away. Don't do it.

This is serious stuff. As a Christian friend, a man, and a pastor, I want to tell you that if you have issues in your life, we're here to help you. In the last year and a half we've done two conferences dealing with sexual brokenness, sexual immorality, and homosexuality. I want to introduce Dr. David Foster, one of the foremost authorities on this subject. He has done support groups for people who are struggling with these issues. He has a great television show and a website, www.purepassion.us. He is an ordained minister of this church. He's a man who came out of a sexually immoral lifestyle, and for the last twenty-five plus years has lived victoriously with Jesus Christ.

I want to say this again: we don't hate people, and we're not mad at people. We're not here to throw stones. We're here to lead people to Jesus Christ. We are not here to soft pedal or whitewash or condone what people are doing, whether it is homosexuality or getting high. We're not whitewashing anything. But in a day when this topic is so red hot and there is so much confusion, we needed to clearly speak out about it.

We want to offer people hope and help in the person of Jesus Christ. You can come to me, send me an e-mail, come to the pastoral staff, or come to David—he has a heart for people. We will treat your situation in confidence. We're not going to be surprised, we're not going to be shocked, we're not going to condemn you. We want to give you tools to help you. We want to see you become whole.

Please, don't take your strides from the media, don't take your opinions from heretical, backslidden blasphemers and preachers who are leading people to hell. Don't take your cues from them. Don't do that. Listen to what God's Word says. Follow Jesus, love Him, serve Him, and watch Him do in your life what only He can do. We need to be a holy people; we need to be a pure people. He asks us to, and because He asks, it means He gives us the grace to do it. Let's not whitewash our sin. Let's get right with God. Let's be a holy habitation for His presence.

• • • • • • • • • • • • • • • • • •

Part 4

The church at Sardis

4

PREFACE

Let's review what we've already studied about the churches that received letters from Jesus. We started with the church of Ephesus and learned that they were the loveless church. They were the church that left their first love and became very mechanical and religious. They were doing their Christianity without Christ. Then we examined the church of Smyrna, the persecuted church. Jesus promised them that they would be thrown into prison and that Satan would tempt and test them. They had gone through a really rough time, and they were going to go through another rough time. Then, we unpacked the letters to the churches of Pergamos and Thyatira. Jesus rebuked them both for devilish compromise and sexual immorality. It was a pretty sobering and heavy message.

In the third chapter of Revelation, we're going to take a look at the letter to the church of Sardis. Jesus had some interesting things to say to them. He actually had nothing positive—not one good thing—to say about the corporate church. It brings me to tears. When I prepare to preach about this kind of passage, there's a war that goes on in me about what I know needs to be said. It keeps me up at night. My flesh says, "Dude, are you sure you're going to say that?" But I am going to say it, because I know that if we hear it, it'll change our lives forever. I'm realizing more and more all the time, as a believer and as a preacher, how important it is that I say what God tells me to say and then let the chips fall where they will. So here's the message, a strong message from Jesus, in all love and truth.

Jesus is concerned about us all the time. In light of that and in that spirit, I want to say that Jesus has something to say to us in this letter. For some of us, it might be like He's got the cat o' nine tails out. For some of us, it might be like He's turning our tables over and throwing our money out the door or challenging and correcting us. But we have to remember that the reason He's doing it is because He loves us too much to leave us like we are. He's concerned. After we hear His message, we need to respond with, "Okay, Jesus, I see what you're saying. There's truth in what you're saying and now I'm going to respond appropriately." May God do that work in us as we study this letter.

BACKGROUND

Sardis was an extremely wealthy city, and it had all kinds of fun little things about it. For example, the first coins were actually minted in Sardis. At the time this book was written, the richest man in the whole world lived in Sardis. It was the carpet capital of the world. There was a lot of commerce and trade, and it was booming. It was a very, very wealthy economy and city.

It was also a very safe and secure place because Sardis sat atop a hill. People looked at it like it could never be overcome. They thought it could never be penetrated or defeated. Never say "never" though, right?

It was a wealthy city that was very secure. I want you to think about that for a second. Are you with me? If you had all kinds of cash, and you were very secure in your cash and who you were, what temptations do you think would prompt you to be distant from Christ? What attitudes in your heart might well up to keep you distant from Christ? The believers in Sardis were complacent. They comforted themselves right into death while they were going to church. They put other things than Christ in their minds.

• • • • • • • • • • • • • • • • •

THE MESSAGE TO THE CHURCH IN SARDIS

Let's see what Jesus had to say to this church that had fallen captive to its own wealth and security in Revelation 3:1–6:

> "To the angel of the church in Sardis write, 'These things says He who has the seven Spirits of God and the seven stars: "I know your works, that you have a name that you are alive, but you are dead. Be watchful, and strengthen the things which remain, that are ready to die, for I have not found your works perfect before God. Remember therefore how you have received and heard; hold fast and repent. Therefore if you will not watch, I will come upon you like a thief, and you will not know what hour I will come upon you. You have a few names even in Sardis who have not defiled their garments; and they shall walk with Me in white, for they are worthy. He who overcomes shall be clothed in white garments, and I will not blot out his name from the Book of Life, but I will confess his name before my Father and before His angels. He who has an ear, let him hear what the Spirit says to the churches."'"
>
> Revelation 3:1–6

Save those few undefiled saints Jesus mentioned in verse four, He didn't have one good thing to say to the church in Sardis. Amazing

JESUS' TITLE: THE SEVEN SPIRITS OF GOD

We will start unpacking this letter by noticing the title that Jesus uses for Himself. The title He uses says everything. This is radically important and it's going to take us a few steps to get there, so hold on.

Many of us know from Scripture that the number seven always refers to completeness or perfection. When Jesus calls Himself "He who has the seven Spirits of God" in Revelation 3:1, what He is saying is, "I am He who is perfect and complete. I have the fullness of the Holy Spirit. There is nothing that I am lacking. I am everything that the Holy Spirit has to offer; it is found in Me."

Let's look at Isaiah 11:2:

> "The Spirit of the Lord shall rest upon Him, the Spirit of wisdom and understanding, the Spirit of counsel and might, the Spirit of knowledge and of the fear of the Lord."
>
> Isaiah 11:2

There are seven things right there. Most commentators believe that the seven aspects referred to in the sevenfold Spirit of Jesus are seen here in Isaiah. He has the fullness and the completeness of the Spirit. You're thinking, "Okay, Steve that's great. What else?" Well, it's imperative that we understand what the Spirit gives us, in the most general sense, because that plays a part in this teaching. Jesus is full of the Spirit. He's got the completeness of the Spirit.

Here's a question: What is it essentially that the Spirit gives us? The answer is LIFE. The Spirit gives us life. He corrects and convicts us, among other things, but the ultimate, big-picture idea is that the Holy Spirit gives us life. Zoe is the Greek word for life. It's spiritual life. It's eternal life. It's a life that isn't in you prior to the Holy Spirit coming and touching your spirit. We used to be dead in our trespasses and sins, but the Spirit has come and given us life.

Jesus told his disciples, "It is the Spirit who gives life; the flesh profits nothing. The words that I speak to you are spirit, and they are life" (*John 6:63*). There's a connection between spirit and life. Paul writes in Romans 8:11 that "if the Spirit of Him who raised Jesus from the dead dwells in you, He who raised Christ from the dead will also give life to your mortal bodies through His Spirit who dwells in you."

Jesus refers to Himself as the One who has the fullness or completeness of the Spirit. We also understand that the Spirit's job is to give us life. So the reason Jesus calls Himself "He who has the seven Spirits of God" is that He's laying down His credentials for what He's about to say to them. He says, "I know what life is. I know what Spirit is. I've got both: Spirit and Life, Eternal God in Me. I am fully qualified to judge life from death. I know the difference."

SARDIS' CONDITION: DEAD AND RESTING

Jesus said in Revelation 2:1,

"Hey, I am He who walks through the midst of the seven lampstands which are the seven churches." Jesus was there in the midst of His churches, walking around, looking at what was going on. He told the people of Sardis in Revelation 3:1, "Hey, I know your works. I know you have a name that you're alive, but I've been checking you all out and you all are dead." He used the word for corpse. He said to the church people, "I've been looking at you. I'm Spirit. I'm Life. I'm fully able to judge and discern this— I know the difference between life and death. I've been checking you out, and you all are dead."

Have you ever been to a dead church? Europe is full of them. They're becoming mosques by the day. They're empty. They're called "the tombs of God" because they have died on the vine. They quit their intimate relationship with Jesus Christ. They slowly decayed as they ventured into religion and away from a relationship with Christ that was vibrant and real. Jesus said to Sardis, "I'm He who has the seven Spirits of God. I know life when I see it, and it ain't here." When they heard that, there was a serious gulp. Whoa.

I am sure they sat there and said, "But we're Christians! We go to the church of Sardis. We don't sleep in on Sunday mornings. Ah, come on! What else, what else, what else? Come up with something. Say something."

There's nothing Jesus could say. It's difficult to talk to dead men. It's a very serious assessment.

What happened to them? How did the church in Sardis become this way? We don't know exactly. We look back and understand that they were wealthy and secure, they became complacent unto death, and they became self-sufficient. Looking back, I think we can paint a pretty clear picture of what happened. I think it's safe to say that they had substituted wealth and security for spiritual life while they were going to church. They had become about "going to" church instead of "being" the church. They had comfort that led to complacency. Their complacency led to spiritual death. They felt that they had so much and they didn't need God.

Jesus said something else interesting to Sardis. He said, "You have a name that you are alive, but you are dead" (*Rev. 3:1*). They were a resting church. Were they resting on their successful past reputation? Did they have a name so great that when people said "Sardis" they said, "Oo, the church of Sardis...wow!"?

What Jesus sees isn't what people see. He looks much deeper. He looks at the heart. He doesn't just look at the action. Were they resting on their reputation? Were they resting on their history? Were they resting on an aging altar call that had happened to them years back? Were they resting on an answered prayer that had happened years ago, but nothing recent? Had it been years since they had been successfully used by God to expand the kingdom, and they were still looking back?

I remember the days when our church met in the cafeteria. I remember when we moved to the gym. I remember when we moved to this campus. Here we are, thousands of people later, with a beautiful campus. Beloved, we're in big trouble if we're looking back—big trouble. Is that what happened to Sardis?

It's what has happened historically to entire denominations. They were birthed out of revival's fire—the Spirit of God came down and raised up leaders, giving them boldness to preach and touch people's hearts. As a result, thousands got saved. They established mission societies and Bible literature societies and got the Word of God out there. But slowly, slowly, slowly, things got cold, lukewarm, irrelevant, and unreal. Entire denominations find themselves today like the church at Sardis—dead and resting.

We mentioned in the last lesson some of the various churches that have given themselves over to sexual immorality and devilish compromise. I don't mean to pick on one in particular, but I just have to mention the Methodist Church because their founders—George Whitefield and the Wesley brothers—were so fervent with the fire of God. I'd say those men are rolling over in their graves because of what's happening in the Methodist Church they founded. They were first called Methodist because of their method of seeking God so passionately every single day. Their checklist of things they kept account of every day—rules and just pressing into God—was fantastic. The denomination started there, and now, years later, it's approving sexually immoral behavior. Whew! Serious stuff. They have a name that is alive, but they are dead and resting on their past achievements.

In the church in Sardis, the Spirit was quenched. The Spirit was resisted. The Spirit was no longer wanted or welcomed. Rather, He was discarded and they didn't depend on Him. Consequently, death ruled where life should have, and once did, rule.

Beloved, we've got to make sure of some things as believers, individually and corporately. We have to make sure that we never let anything about our reputation or our history quench our desperate need for the Holy Spirit's life today, right now. We have to make sure that we never let our comfort lead to complacency, which ultimately leads to death. We have to never stop hungering for the Spirit's presence in our midst. I'm telling you it is possible to slide backwards, and I will go beyond that and say it is probable, if we don't do regular checkups.

What concerns me right now is what I see going on all over the place, in the name of Jesus, in the name of Christianity, and in the name of church, that is so "un-Jesus" and so "un-first-century-church." It's my personal struggle right now. I'm getting consumed with it. I'm getting frustrated with God, to be honest with you, because I don't know what else to do. I don't know any other prayers to pray. I don't know how much more pacing, begging, and weeping I can do. Man, we've got everything in the world to be thankful for right here. There are preachers out in the nation that would give their right eye to have my job and pastor this church. But none of that is important. If people aren't coming to Christ and disciples aren't being raised up, I couldn't care less how many people come here. I couldn't care less how big the offerings are. Beloved, this isn't about becoming a country club. This isn't about us just sitting back and getting complacent and comfortable in our ever-expanding everything. This is about each of us asking, "Do I have a name that I'm alive but really I'm dead?"

I really think part of the struggle I've had leading up to giving this message is that God gave me a little bit of the taste of what dead people feel like, and I can't stand it. That feeling is contrary to everything that Jesus is in my heart. When I think about how there are people who come to this church who are dead inside, I don't know what to do about it. I don't know how I can preach any more. I don't know how to pray any more. I don't know what else to do. I just beg you: please, will you get right with Jesus? I'm not mad at you. I'm not judging you. I'm not condemning you. Jesus isn't condemning you. He's asking you: "Will you get right with Me?"

Too many times we come up with things that are only about guilting people into right behavior. "Are you reading your Bible? Are you saying your prayers? And are you witnessing for Jesus?" And you respond with, "Well, no, not as much as I should . . . and, okay, now I feel guilty. And now I'm going to get better. Now I'm going to try harder." Do you know how long that lasts? Two weeks. You see, beloved, this message isn't about guilt. This message isn't about shaming anybody. This message is about reality and life. Do you have life in you?

Is there something in your heart that says, "I love reading God's Word"? Someone with life would say, "It's beautiful. It's like honey in my mouth. I love the Word of God. It lights my path. It gives me wisdom. It gives me life. It gives me strength. It gives me hope. You don't have to tell me to read my Bible, Pastor; you'd have to tear it out of my hands."

Do you love praying? Do you look forward to spending time with Him? Does your heart beat for Him, like your lover? After Jesus' death, Mary stood outside His tomb, weeping with a heart asking, "Where can I go and find Him? Where have they taken Him?" (*see John 10:11–13*). You see, she was so used to wanting Him and being around Him that even at His death, she had to draw near. I'm not trying to make you feel guilty, I'm just asking you: does your heart beat for Him? Do you love His presence? Do you love the thrill of being able to share who Jesus is to you with people that don't know Him? Do you look for opportunities because you know the world's going to hell in a handbasket? Do you speak a word of truth to somebody who could use it? It doesn't matter if anybody is watching. It doesn't matter if no one but Jesus will ever know. Does your heart beat to share the love of the Son of God with people? Do you love His presence? Do you love His Word? I'm not being a legalist; I'm just saying that if that's not your heart, something is wrong. Maybe we have the name that we're alive, but we're dead.

Maybe we're living off of what happened years ago. We may say, "Don't talk to me about my relationship with Christ today—how I'm loving Him, how I'm serving Him. Don't talk about that. I'm still thinking about what happened years ago. I'm living in the faded glory of yesterday. Don't bring up whether I'm sacrificially giving my life, my effort, my time, my talent, and my treasure to God. Don't ask me if I'm doing that today, because—have you forgotten already?—that one time last month, I volunteered in the youth ministry. Don't push me to do more than that."

I love you for serving in the youth ministry, but something tells me that Jesus is worth more than once a month with some snotty-nosed kids. Have we contented ourselves too simply, too easily?

Unfortunately, I can't come up with the official list of things that should be happening in your life and heart to determine whether or not you're spiritually dead. But I don't know how we could say we're spiritually alive if we don't hunger for the truth of God's Word, the beauty of His presence, or the sharing of the Good News. That's not New Testament Christianity. I have read the Book of Acts over and over again and learned what early Christianity was like, and when I see what gets pawned off as Christianity in western civilization today, I think, "Man, there's a huge disconnect." I'm not being mean or self-righteous. Listen, I've got to repent as well. I want to draw nearer to Christ. I read this letter to Sardis, and it causes me to wake up a little bit and say, "Jesus, in our abundance, have we become complacent? In our security, have we become self-sufficient? In our religion, have we become dead? Are we resting on our past?"

SARDIS' RESULT: INCOMPLETE WORKS

The result of their dead condition was that their works weren't perfect or complete before God. Jesus said to them, "Wake up! Strengthen what remains and is about to die, for I have not found your works perfect before God" (*see Rev. 3:2*).

Their works weren't complete. There was work left to do, and they stopped. There were more things to press into. Apparently, they had become content with themselves and with where they had arrived, and they retired from Spirit-led, Spirit-empowered, life-giving service to Christ.

In contrast, Paul said, "I have not arrived, I have not attained it all, but this one thing I do: I press on into the upward call of God in Christ Jesus" (*see Phil. 3:13, 14*). That feeling was absent from the church in Sardis. They had lost that passion and zeal.

But they were in church on Sunday morning. Beloved, when we get complacent and fail to finish the work we're called to do, we'll find something else to do. And that something else, many times, isn't going to be holy. If we're not about our Father's business, we'll find something to be about, and it won't be good. I'm not just talking about the bad sins we think of right away. I'm not saying everybody is going to start doing drugs or sexually immoral things. Our own complacency and apathy is as sinful as anything else we could do.

What happened to the conviction of the sins of omission and not just the sins of commission? We're so settled on the things we're not supposed to do; what about those things we're supposed to do but aren't doing? Do those things trouble our hearts?

The works of the believers in Sardis weren't just incomplete. Their garments were stained by the sins of complacency and self-sufficiency.

JESUS' WARNING

Jesus said, "If you continue to live this way, in this spiritual death, you might be overtaken by Me as a thief. I'll come when you least expect it. That's the consequence for your clueless, complacent spiritual condition" (*see Rev. 3:3*).

He also said something very sobering that smart people have been debating for two thousand years. Jesus' warning to them was not only that their garments were stained and such, but He also said, when referring to those who overcome, "I won't blot their name out of the Book of Life" (*see Rev. 3:5*).

That phrase troubles a lot of people and causes them to ask questions. What about eternal security? What about "once saved, always saved"? This is Jesus talking to church people and He's saying that it is possible for their names to be blotted out of the Book of Life. That makes people nervous! They say, "What's the truth here, Steve? What's the answer? Surely Jesus couldn't mean that!"

I have read commentator after commentator after commentator, each of whom gives his or her best definition of what this means and then says, "But I'm not sure." I've got to tell you, when I read these kinds of passages where Jesus talks this soberly and it looks like Christians who walk away from Him have the ability to lose their salvation, it doesn't concern me at all. Why? Because I'm planning on not being one of those knuckleheads.

It's that simple. If we're worried about our names being blotted out, it's only because we're living dead spiritual lives! When I'm living passionately and purposefully for Jesus, when I'm loving His Word and His presence, when I'm telling people about Him and drawing near to Him in prayer, when I'm fulfilling my ministry, and when the life of His Spirit is present in me and through me, I've got to tell you, I'm not worried about backsliding. I'm not worried about losing my salvation. If that concerns you, then do something about it.

Jesus said, "If you listen to My warning, you won't be blotted out of the Book of Life."

JESUS' SOLUTION

Wake Up

Jesus' solution for these folks, really simply, was to be watchful. It literally means they needed to wake up. He said, "You need to wake up and get up out of the slumber!" (*see Rev. 3:2*). We need to listen to what's being said. We need to do spiritual inventory. We need to check and see if this applies to us. It doesn't matter who you are or how old you are or what other people will think. If you feel you are dead inside right now, come clean and get life, because He offers it.

No preacher or teacher can solve this for us. We need to come to the altar and say, "Jesus, I need You right here, right now." Then, it's about waking up Monday morning and saying the same thing! That doesn't mean that today isn't enough for the rest of my life. Today, right now, is permission and access to get everything we need from Him for the rest of our lives. Today we can build a loving relationship, receive from Him, get everything He has to offer, and move on. There is no microwave, instant-satisfaction kind of Christianity. There is no drive-thru, one-time fix-it-all, ninety-nine-cent meal deal. When we come to Christ and make it real, it's about every single day—not about looking back. Oh yeah, I remember when I got baptized out at the ocean. Oh man, that was the greatest thing. I just wanted to park there for the next twenty-five years. But I couldn't do that. I got baptized in the ocean to become a fireplug for God for the next twenty-five years! Jesus says, "Every day, wake up and be watchful."

Strengthen What Remains

When Jesus said in verse 2, "Strengthen the things which remain," He was telling them, "You're dead, man, but there's a little bit left." I love something that the prophet Isaiah said about Jesus: "Smoking flax He will not quench" (*Is. 42:3*). It means even if there's just a little bit of smoke left in your spirit that once was on fire for God, Jesus' desire isn't to quench it and put it out and blow you off. His desire is to fan what's left into flame. His desire is to say, "Come on, come on. Here you go . . . now you're going. Come on, come on, come on, come on." If you'll just say, "Yes, Jesus I need You to breathe on me. Breathe Your life on me—in me and through me. I need You." Smoking flax He will not quench. That's His desire. It's what He wants to do. If we've been dead and complacent, there's still time to strengthen what remains.

Hold Fast

Jesus also said, "Watch out" (*see Rev. 3:2*). He doesn't just say wake up, but also watch out. He's asking them to pay attention to what's going on. He's asking them to not let this moment pass. If you're dead in your spirit, please get right with God. And then hold fast and hold on.

Turn Back

Jesus also told them to remember how they received life and heard truth from Him and asked them to repent. He wanted them to turn back to Him. Remember what it used to be like—assuming you have a "what it used to be like"—and return to Him.

Jesus' Hope

Jesus had hope for the believers in Sardis. He said, "Man, you all can be clothed in white. You can be pure and holy and spotless and blameless and stainless. You don't have to have your garments stained by the sins of complacency, self-sufficiency, and death. You can walk with Me. I'll walk with you." Then He said, "I will confess your name before My Father and the angels in heaven. I will confess your name" (*see Rev. 3:4, 5*).

Jesus told them to be overcomers. He told them to just get over this place of spiritual death they were in. He wanted them to get off that treadmill they'd been on. You know what I mean—you do well for six weeks and then tank for six years, you do well for six weeks and then tank for six years. He said, "Get off of that." He implored them to be overcomers so that He could confess them before the Father in heaven. Wow, that's hope.

There is always hope for the wayward Christian, but you have to respond with obedience to the call of Jesus to wake up, strengthen what remains, watch out, hold fast, remember what you've received from Him, repent, and turn back to Him.

There's always hope.

WHERE ARE YOU TODAY?

Has something happened in your spiritual life that has caused you to have a name that you're alive, but you're really dead? Have abundance and complacency slipped in? Will you repent?

I don't have a magic wand to wave over you. I can't fix it; only you can. Today can be the day of your fresh start with Jesus. Today you can say, "Lord, I don't know how that death crept in, but I know how I can get rid of it." This is a message for all people. It's a message for high schoolers, young adults, and old folks like me. Are you alive in Jesus today? Does your heart beat for His Word and His presence and His face? Are you loving Him well, above all else? Or is it just religion? Remember, Jesus said these words to a church—wow!

Here's a warning: it's so important in times like this that you're not responding in guilt or just being touched at an emotional or mental level. It's really important that you are responding in the Spirit, saying:

Lord, today is a marked day in my spiritual journey. This is a day where I am trading death for life. This is a day when I'm not going back to business as usual, but I am pressing onward and upward into the higher call of God for my life. This is the day I will not be content with what I've accomplished in my past. I'm going to press into You, Jesus, and into everything that You have for me. Forgive me for my complacency. Forgive me for my self-sufficiency. I am desperate for Your Spirit. And I am desperate for life. No games. No excuses. No emotion. Just spiritual truth.

You're loved in Christ Jesus.

••••••••••••••••••

Part 5

The church at Philadelphia

5

PREFACE

*T*he next letter in Revelation 3 is addressed to the church at Philadelphia, and it has some very encouraging words. I hope that after you finish reading this section you will have a fresh vision of what it means to be a passionate and equipped servant of Jesus Christ—that's one important facet of this teaching. I hope you'll look into your life and say, "Okay, God, that means me. I'm not going to let this only be said of the church at Philadelphia; I'm going to own this myself. I want what is said about them to be said about me, so I am going to incorporate this teaching into my life." This lesson should be radically encouraging and should birth some big vision in all of us.

We're going to break this letter into five parts:

- The Authority of Jesus Christ
- The Opening of Jesus Christ
- The Promise of Jesus Christ
- The Exhortation of Jesus Christ, and
- The Reward of Jesus Christ.

BACKGROUND

The city of Philadelphia was the city of brotherly love. It was a young city, less than two hundred years old, founded in 150 B.C. by Attalus II. It was an outpost or frontier city that kept barbarians and raiders from entering Asia Minor. The Philadelphians were kind of like the dangling dog bone for the barbarians, who would hit Philadelphia first so Sardis, Ephesus, and the greater, mightier cities could get ready for what was coming their way. Philadelphia was leveled, as was Sardis, by a huge earthquake and was rebuilt in 17 A.D.

THE MESSAGE TO THE CHURCH AT PHILADELPHIA

Let's look at Revelation 3:7–13. This is Jesus speaking to us and to the church at Philadelphia:

"And to the angel of the church in Philadelphia write,'These things says He who is holy, He who is true, "He who has the key of David, He who opens and no one shuts, and shuts and no one opens": "I know your works. See, I have set before you an open door, and no one can shut it; for you have a little strength, have kept My word, and have not denied My name. Indeed I will make those of the synagogue of Satan, who say they are Jews and are not, but lie—indeed I will make them come and worship before your feet, and to know that I have loved you. Because you have kept My command to persevere, I also will keep you from the hour of trial which shall come upon the whole world, to test those who dwell on the earth. Behold, I am coming quickly! Hold fast what you have, that no one may take your crown. He who overcomes, I will make him a pillar in the temple of My God, and he shall go out no more. I will write on him the name of My God and the name of the city of My God, the New Jerusalem, which comes down out of heaven from My God. And I will write on him My new name. He who has an ear, let him hear what the Spirit says to the churches.""

Revelation 3:7–13

THE AUTHORITY

Jesus began His message to the Philadelphians in verse 7 by proving His authority. He said, "I am He who holds the very key of David." The key of David is first mentioned in Isaiah 22:22 in reference to the scribe, or the keeper of the king's stuff. This person had the key to the treasury. He had access to all of the king's resources; he could open the king's resources at any time and distribute them any way he liked. He also could shut up the king's treasury and lock it up so nobody could get in. With this statement in verse 7, Jesus was saying, "I am He who is in charge of the vast spiritual riches of the almighty God."

Jesus was getting ready to open some of those glorious treasures—kingdom opportunities—to the church in Philadelphia. He let them know upfront that no one could shut a door He opens. He said, "I'm the One who opens it, and I'm the One who closes it; nobody has a say in it except Me." He was talking about His absolute authority. Thank Jesus that He's in charge!

THE OPENING

One main idea in this passage that I really want you to catch is that Jesus opened a door of opportunity to the Philadelphians, and He did it for specific reasons. Let's make some observations about this open door before we get into the reasons why Jesus opened it for them.

Open Door Observations

1. Jesus is the One who opens kingdom doors.

Jesus does it—we don't! It is not our job to open kingdom doors.

2. Jesus is the One who keeps kingdom doors open.

Sometimes we get this confused in our zeal for Christ. We think we need to be zealous and show God we're serious about really going after this thing. We want to finish the ministry, and we want to be obedient. What happens? We bump into the same closed doors every time, and we think if we just hit them harder, they're going to eventually open. But I've got to tell you, closed doors win! We can't try to push them open. It's Jesus' job to open them. Once they are open, we can take stress off of ourselves by thinking, "Okay, Jesus, you opened it. I can take it from here as long as you keep it open."

It's Jesus' job to open the door, and it's Jesus' job to keep it open. It's our job to live in the Spirit, to flow with His Spirit, and to simply walk through open doors. It's our job to welcome those into our presence who walk through the door toward us. It's that simple. Quit trying to kick the door down. Quit trying to make things happen in your own strength. Don't give birth to any Ishmaels[1]—they've caused problems for centuries. Just let Jesus open the door and do what He does.

3. We must recognize open doors.

Paul understood this issue of open doors—big time. This is a spiritual principle, not just some natural slogan to add to some distant spiritual concept. This is the truth of God. This is how God opens doors at the right time with the right people to accommodate and accomplish His kingdom purposes. In 2 Corinthians 2:12, Paul wrote about a time when he "came to Troas to preach Christ's gospel, and a door was opened to [him] by the Lord." It was the Lord who did it. It wasn't Paul saying, "Hey, I think I'm going to Troas to preach the gospel." No, he walked in the Spirit and was led by the Spirit. When he arrived at the place the Spirit led him, he realized that God had opened a door. There was an opportunity. See, it's easy. It's about getting into the flow. It's about listening. It's about finding where God is working and joining Him instead of trying to do our own thing—attempting to open our own doors and then saying, "Now, God, come down here and bless this."

Paul made this observation in 1 Corinthians 16:9: "A great and effective door has opened to me, and there are many adversaries." The Lord is the One who opens doors, and we must be people who recognize open doors. Paul realized that something was going on around him. He had his spiritual sight right and could see God working. He said, "God, You're doing something right here, right now. You've opened this door and You want me to walk through it with Your power and Your authority and Your love and Your hope and Your gospel, and You're going to impact people through this. There is a great and effective door right here, God, and I'm going to walk through because You've opened it."

Paul also let us know that adversaries may come with open doors. In fact, they're usually there on the other side saying, "Are you sure you want to walk through this? Are you sure you have what it takes to do this?" But far be it from us to shrink back and stay in the place of comfort and complacency.

We've got to recognize Jesus' open doors. We have to be spiritually in tune with Him so we can realize that what is happening around us isn't some natural thing—some coincidence or random circumstance. Jesus is working right then and there.

I went out to dinner recently with a male friend of mine, and something interesting happened. In the midst of our dinner, our waitress let us know that she thought my friend and I were an item. Now, I must admit, we were looking pretty good. But my thought was, "I believe the Lord is opening a door right here." The night progressed, and she made another comment. Then one of us said, "Both of us have been happily married for a long time. We each have kids!" It became a little joke between the three of us.

Then I realized that there was an opportunity for the gospel right at that moment. The Lord opened the door. We didn't have to try to kick it down ourselves and have her sit down and listen to the Four Spiritual Laws. As she made her rounds, she asked how long we each had been married. My friend said thirty-something years, and I said almost twenty-two years. She asked,

"What's the secret to a long, happy marriage?" Now there's an open door!

My point is, there are open doors in restaurants. There are open doors in the frozen food aisle. There are open doors with the guy who comes to jump-start your car because you left your lights on. There are open doors with your neighbors. There are open doors all the time! We just need to be spiritually sensitive and have spiritual vision to see God working right there in front of us.

I'm a guy who loves to get involved in what God's doing, so I responded to the waitress's question. I said, "Get ready to hear something that is going to make your jaw hit the floor." She said, "What is it?" I told her, "The key to a long, successful marriage is that you have to love Jesus first and foremost, above all else, and then, and only then, will you learn to love your spouse effectively."

I don't think God opened up that opportunity so I would have a good illustration for this teaching. She looked and me and said, "That's the last thing I thought you were going to tell me." You see, she got a little dose of Jesus that night. While she served us a little Italian food, she got a little taste of kingdom food. She was surprised because the Lord wanted to do a work in her life and opened the door. Now she knows the secret of having a happy marriage is loving the Lord Jesus Christ first and foremost.

That was an easy little thing—an easy little open door to walk through. But what about bigger things? What about those doors that are not just personal doors for you to walk through? What about things here at this church? You need to know that we have kingdom eyes here. We are looking for open doors. We are looking for people and places and things and opportunities all around the world. It doesn't mean that everything that comes our way is an opportunity or open door from God. Sometimes it's just a good idea, not a "God idea." Consequently, we sift through those things. For example, we have seen our work with the orphans in China as an open door through relationships and things that have come our way, and we have been prayerful about it. We've said, "God, You're doing something here and we want in." That's been the pattern throughout our history as we've joined God's work in Africa, Haiti, Sri Lanka, Mexico, or anywhere else.

We saw the door open with Narrow Gate. Initially it was just this room full of three or four smelly guys looking at me saying, "Teach us the Bible, because Bill and Stacy are busy doing computer work. What do you have to say to that?" That's an open door. Here are some hungry young guys. Let's dive in and help them, support them, buy them some Bibles, and show them the love of Christ. Look at what God has done over the last four years. Today, Narrow Gate has their own lodge and countless young men have graduated from it. Bill and Stacy are doing full-time ministry, and it just continues to grow and grow. It's because we have kingdom eyes. We see open doors and we jump in. We don't always do it because we feel the most qualified or because we've got so much money we don't know what to do with it. A lot of times, we feel inferior and incapable of doing what God wants. But we've chosen to trust Him because He's opened the door and He continues to keep the door open. It's true for me personally, and it's true for you personally. It's true for us corporately. Jesus is into opening doors. He is into expanding His church and doing greater things through His people all the time!

4. We must pray for open doors.

Paul asked the Colossians to pray "that God would open to us a door for the word, to speak the mystery of Christ" (*Col. 4:3*). So here's another thing about open doors: we are to pray for them! We should say, "Jesus, You do it. I want to be sensitive to Your leading. I want to recognize an opportunity from You and respond to it appropriately." We need to personally and corporately ask Jesus to open more doors for us to speak His Word. What might happen if each person in this church was praying, "God, would you open a door for me to speak the gospel? God, I don't want to just hear about Pastor Steve's experience at the restaurant; I want to have my own experience at the restaurant. Jesus, today, open a door for me that I might speak Your Word and communicate the mystery of Christ to someone."

I heard something that was really sweet just before the first service: "The Holy Spirit in you is for you. The Holy Spirit upon you is for other people." Jesus told His disciples, "When the Holy Spirit has come upon you . . . you shall be witnesses to Me" (*Acts 1:8*). Tomorrow morning, you could say, "Lord, with the Holy Spirit upon me, let me be a witness to somebody else. Would you open the door for me to speak the Word of Christ? Lord, I want to recognize it; help me see it. Lord, I want to walk in it; I want to respond appropriately. I want to see You touch somebody's life. Will You open the door?"

You know, Jesus has an open door policy: pray for it, recognize it, receive it, respond to it, and walk in it. Keep asking Him to open those doors and to work through you personally and all of us corporately.

WHY JESUS CHOSE PHILADELPHIA

In Revelation 3:8, Jesus said He was going to open a door for the Philadelphians that nobody could shut. Why? Three reasons are given in the same verse.

1. They had little strength in themselves.

He wasn't getting down on them by saying, "You have a little strength." He wasn't making fun of them or condemning them. He was saying, "I'm going to open this door for you because you have little strength compared to Me." He would do something for them that they couldn't do for themselves. Even with Christ in them, with their hope of glory, and with everything else God had blessed them with, they still didn't have the ability to open up these spiritual doors. Again, that's always Jesus' job. He said to them, "Because you have little strength, I'm going to do this for you."

I love how this shows that we are truly co-laborers with Christ. He opens the door because we have little strength. Have you ever opened a door for a struggling little kid? Isn't it a blast when you get to walk over in your big adult strength and open the door for them, and watch them run through it with joy? I love that. I love being able to open doors for people. Jesus said, "Because you have little strength, I'm going to open this door for you and nobody's going to be able to shut it." I love the security of that. That's awesome.

2. They kept His Word.

The believers in Philadelphia had a high regard for the Word of God. They didn't compromise it. They believed it, they studied it, they taught it, and they lived it.

The Holy Spirit said expressly that in the last days, in which we now live, people "will depart from the faith, giving heed to deceiving spirits and doctrines of demons" (*1 Tim. 4:1*). He said people will be pulled away from the Word of God. They'll heap up for themselves false teachers who will scratch their itching theological ears. They'll pay pastors big salaries so the people can hear the kind of doctrine they want to hear and nothing else (*2 Tim. 4:3*). In these last days, when entire denominations have left the Word of God behind, we, like the Philadelphians of old, have to be people who keep the Word of God. We have to be people who hold it in high regard, realizing that God has magnified His Word above His own name (*Ps. 138:2*). The Bible is radically important. You can't do life without it.

Treasuring it the right way, however, means keeping your balance on a tightrope. Some people are only interested in the print of the Word and not in the Person of the Word. Unfortunately, people only interested in the print just become mean-spirited, Bible-know-it-all, self-appointed doctrine police. On the other side, there are people who have thrown out the Word of God and are into what they refer to as "the spirit"—and anything goes in the spirit. They end up doing things in the so-called spirit that have no root in the Word of God, and just because they are cosmic and mystic, everybody goes, "Ooo." So what should we be doing? We need have the Holy Spirit and God's written truth—a healthy balance of both. ·

We shouldn't write and sing songs that sound mystical and wonderful and spiritual and all that but are full of bad doctrine. Just because they reach somebody emotionally doesn't mean they are filled with good, sound doctrine and speak truth from the Word of God.

The days in which we live are interesting. I'm not willing to be all about head knowledge, and I'm not willing to be out there on some limb they call "the spirit" that has no root in the Word; I want both. I want the best of both worlds. I want to study, show myself approved, and rightly divide the Word of Truth. I want the Word to be life to me and the reason I have hope. I want to know what I believe and why I believe it. I want to memorize it. I want to be able to share the gospel and give reasons for what I believe—even if I don't have my Bible with me. Even if it isn't in my hand, it's in my heart—I want to know it that well. I want to be filled and anointed with the Spirit of God. Every day I want to be trusting Him and praying, "Lord, fill me afresh. Fill me anew for what's going on in my life." I want both the Word and the Spirit.

The Philadelphians had little strength and they kept Jesus' Word. We need to make the most of every opportunity that comes our way—every open door to get into the truth of God's Word.

3. They didn't deny His name.

In doctrine and in deeds, the Philadelphians held fast to the teaching and the Person of Jesus Christ. They lived what they believed and believed what they lived. There was no contradiction between their confession and their profession and their lifestyle. It was all one and the same. How they lived matched up with how they talked.

What is "denying His name"? It's living like a jerk while you say you love Jesus. It's a denial of His character, and it's a denial of His cause. Jesus said to the Philadelphians, "You have little strength, but you've kept My word and you haven't denied My name. Because you have been faithful, trustworthy disciples of Mine—the real deal—I'm going to do something amazing in you and through you."

Jesus was about to open an awesome kingdom door for them because they could be trusted. Their history proved it. The way they lived and operated in the Spirit showed it. Jesus saw them as people who could steward the opening of a door very well—people who would not embarrass the King or the kingdom by fumbling and dropping the ball.

I want to be a good investment for Jesus. I want Him to look at my life and say, "Berger is an interesting fellow, but I've got to say this about him: he hasn't denied Me, he has kept My Word, and he hasn't compromised." I want Him to be able to say, "Because your history shows that you are a faithful man, I'm going to trust you with more. You're a good investment. With the little bit of strength that you had, you did all you could do."

FAITHFULNESS IN SMALL BEGINNINGS

Some of us think that if we had more, we would be more. What have we done with the one talent we were given? But we say, "I want ten!" Essentially, we haven't earned it. We want to have a ministry. We want to be part of something big, and we want to head it up, but we haven't learned how to wash a toilet yet. We want to go to the nations, but we haven't shared Christ with the person who lives next door. We're hoping for something bigger and better, but we haven't proven ourselves to be a good investment. We've got to show that we are faithful. We cannot deny His name.

A friend of mine, Dr. Mark Rutland, told me a story from when he was a young evangelist traveling around in his car. He kept his clothes in a worn-out cardboard box in his trunk, and he'd travel for weeks at a time without seeing his family. He was dead broke, had nothing, and often found himself at the end of his rope. One time he visited a church in Georgia in the middle of nowhere, and he got there late after getting lost and going down some old red-clay road. It was this worn-out little church building that literally had stakes around it propping it up. He went up to the window and looked inside, and to his dismay, he saw only a few people. There was this ancient eighty-five-year-old doing nothing. There was somebody banging out an old lifeless hymn on the piano. Nobody seemed to care about being there. The last thing Mark wanted to do was go inside that church. But he told me, "If I ever heard God, I heard Him speak to me right there in the juniper bush. God said, 'Mark, if you're too big to speak to these six people, you are too small to speak to six thousand.'"

Let's not despise the days of small beginnings. Let's be faithful in little, as Jesus said, and be made ruler over much. Let's not try to start at the top, because when we start at the bottom and work our way up, we learn everything we need to learn about handling the challenges and blessings that come with successful ministry. Let's keep in mind what the master said to the faithful servant in Jesus' parable of the talents:

> "Well done, good and faithful servant; you were faithful over a few things, I will make you ruler over many things. Enter into the joy of your lord"
>
> Matthew 25:21

Jesus was about to open an awesome kingdom door for the Philadelphians because they could be trusted. Their history said they would steward the opening well and not embarrass the kingdom. They would do the right thing if they had more, and Jesus knew it. So He wanted to open a door that would blow people's minds.

Let's go back to the letter to the church at Philadelphia and look at verse 9. It says: "I will make those of the synagogue of Satan who say that they are Jews and are not, but lie—indeed, I will make them come and worship before your feet, and to know that I have loved you."

There are two opinions about this. Some people say, "This means that Jesus is going to drag those pagan, Satan-worshiping, false Jews to the feet of the Christians, and they're going to worship at the feet of the Christians. They will finally have to admit that Jesus' love is real." That's one viewpoint. But I don't believe this passage is about believers being vindicated, because we're not in the position to judge. No, this isn't about believers' vindication; it's all about unbelievers' salvation!

I believe Jesus' message to this group of really faithful people who have kept His Word and not denied His name is this: "I'm going to open a door for the people that you least expected—pagan Satan-worshipers—to come through. I'm going to have them come in where you are waiting and give them salvation. They are going to fall at your feet, but they won't be worshiping you. You all will worship Me together. They are going to admit that the love of God is real and that it has touched their hearts."

The Philadelphians were a good investment. They were genuine Christians, and they lived a right lifestyle. Jesus said, "I'm going to start bringing people through those doors, because when they get in the midst of your spiritual health, it's going to be a good, safe place for them. They are going to come to know Me and experience My love in your midst."

What greater privilege could there be? What greater honor could be given to a church than for Jesus to look at them and say, "You guys have got it going on. You're getting it right. This is a great place for people to come. Open up the doors—I'm sending them. Get ready to love them well." What greater honor could a church receive? I believe this passage is all about, and only about, exactly that. These believers were faithful, and Jesus was sending people—the last people they would have ever guessed—to come and be saved.

It's always good to have the Bible to back up your beliefs. So I thought, When has there been an occurrence of the most unlikely person getting saved, and someone from the church was right there, anointed by the Spirit, ready to meet his or her needs and win this person to Christ? Well, that guy Saul of Tarsus came to mind. He confessed to be a Jew and was so passionate about the traditions of his fathers that he went around persecuting, imprisoning, binding, and murdering Christians. If anybody was never going to get saved, it was Saul of Tarsus! But God had a "Philadelphian" He wanted to use in Saul's life, and his name was Ananias. He was cautious, yet anointed. While God was working on Saul of Tarsus, He was also simultaneously preparing Ananias's heart to receive a person who was as lost as a ball in high weeds. Ananias probably thought of Saul as the last person who would ever come to Christ. But Ananias ended up receiving him, welcoming him, walking through that open door, and leading Saul to saving faith.

Do you remember what happened with Saul? He was on the road to Damascus, and Jesus came and knocked him off his high horse. With a bright light all around Him, Jesus said, "Saul, Saul, why are you persecuting Me?" And Saul said, "Uh-oh . . . Jesus?" And Jesus responded, "I am Jesus, whom you are persecuting" (*Acts 9:3–5*).

Let's look at Acts 9:10–18 and see what happened with Saul and Ananias:

> Now there was a certain disciple at Damascus named Ananias; and to him the Lord said in a vision, "Ananias." And he said, "Here I am, Lord." So the Lord said to him, "Arise and go to the street called Straight, and inquire at the house of Judas for one called Saul of Tarsus, for behold, he is praying. And in a vision he has seen a man named Ananias coming in and putting his hand on him, so that he might receive his sight." Then Ananias answered, "Lord, I have heard from many about this man, how much harm he has done to your saints in Jerusalem. And here he has authority from the chief priests to bind all who call on Your name." But the Lord said to him, "Go, for he is a chosen vessel of Mine to bear My name before Gen-

tiles, kings, and the children of Israel. For I will show him how many things he must suffer for My name's sake." And Ananias went his way and entered the house; and laying his hands on him he said, "Brother Saul, the Lord Jesus, who appeared to you on the road as you came, has sent me that you may receive your sight and be filled with the Holy Spirit." Immediately there fell from his eyes something like scales, and he received his sight at once; and he arose and was baptized.

Acts 9:10-18

Jesus is always opening the door for the least likely to come in and receive His love and blessing through an anointed servant of God. It happened with Saul and Ananias. Saul came in and ended up worshiping with the community and becoming Paul, the apostle of God. If we walk in the right way, as the church of Philadelphia did, and if the Lord opens these doors and the surprising people come, let's not be surprised! There are people like Saul of Tarsus out in the world who we see and think, They would never become a believer, when God might be saying, "Hey, they've got a destiny in Me—they just don't know it yet— and these people in My church are arguing with Me about it."

Imagine if some unlikely person walked through our church doors and said, "I hear you guys are real; your testimony is out there. I hear you've got something that I can get and that it will fix my life." Then imagine, after fighting back our own surprise, that we said, "We're so glad to see you! We offer you Christ the King. Receive His salvation." Imagine if that person bowed the knee and worshiped with us. Wow! We'd be just like Philadelphia.

Jesus said, "Because the church at Philadelphia is the real deal, I'm going to open up a door for them." May we remember the open doors come from Jesus. May we recognize them when they come. May we respond appropriately, and may we pray for more of them.

The Philadelphians were about to have the opportunity of ministering to unbelievers who had once been very far off but were coming to the open door of Jesus for salvation! What a privilege, what a miracle! Friends, Jesus wants us to be a church that, even with little strength, keeps His Word and doesn't deny His name, so He can open a door of ministry to us and, through us, bring salvation to the seemingly most unlikely group of people!

THE PROMISE

Returning to our main text, let's reread Revelation 3:10:

> "Because you have kept My command to persevere, I also will keep you from the hour of trial which shall come upon the whole world, to test those who dwell on the earth."
>
> Revelation 3:10

Why should they be kept from the trial? Because they had already passed the test; they didn't need to pass it again. That's why they had been given the privilege of the open door! They had already been found faithful.

Besides, the trial was for "earth dwellers," those who make this world and the things of this world their dwelling place and their desire. That description hardly applies to sold-out believers in Jesus Christ, because sold-out believers in Jesus Christ are strangers and pilgrims here on this earth, and they look for a city whose builder and maker is God (*Heb. 11:10, 13–16*). Their home is heaven and not this earth (*Phil. 3:20*). They are hungry for that. There is no need for faithful believers to go through the Great Tribulation to be tested. They've already passed the test in the Lord Jesus Christ; that's the promise of God.

THE EXHORTATION

Moving on in Revelation 3, let's reread verse 11:

> "Behold, I am coming quickly! Hold fast what you have, that no one may take your crown."
>
> Revelation 3:11

Jesus is coming quickly; hold fast, wake up, and watch out, so no one will take your crown.

Beloved, I am saying, as Jesus did two thousand years ago, that He is coming quickly. "With the Lord one day is as a thousand years, and a thousand years as one day" (*2 Pet. 3:8*). Jesus hasn't even been gone a week yet, and He's coming quickly. We need to live as He said we should—hold fast, wake up, and watch out. Hold on to what you have so that nobody can steal your victor's crown. Don't let anybody take your victor's crown by deception or threatening destruction. Don't let anybody keep you from praising and glorifying and magnifying God. Don't let any person or circumstance take your crown or your song. Do what God's called you to do, keep your eyes on Him, love Him with all you've got, and watch Him come through!

THE REWARD

Finally, let's examine verse 12:

> "He who overcomes, I will make him a pillar in the temple of My God, and he shall go out no more. I will write on him the name of My God and the name of the city of My God, the New Jerusalem, which comes down out of heaven from My God. And I will write on him My new name."
>
> Revelation 3:12

Jesus said overcomers become pillars in the temple of God. It doesn't mean He's turning us to stone. This is a word picture telling us that we will be secure, immovable, planted, and established in the presence of God. It means we'll no longer be wandering, looking for God. Overcomers are established in His very presence! That's got to mean enough to us now to change the way we live here on earth. The hope and reality of heaven has to matter to the saints of God, or we will lose touch with it and become earth-dwellers. God forbid!

He also said that overcomers will be marked by God's name, the name of God's city, and Jesus' new name. They will be marked, owned, and possessed by God, and they will be adopted to be children of God. Overcomers will be entrusted to be His kings and priests, empowered to serve Him and reign with Him. There is nothing greater!

WILL WE BE FAITHFUL LIKE THE CHURCH AT PHILADELPHIA?

We get to choose what kind of people we are. We can be like the church at Sardis, or we can be like the church at Philadelphia. God's not sitting back with a predetermined plan saying, "Oh, you guys are going to stink forever; I've got nothing good to say about you. I don't care how much you pray or what you do, you're just in trouble forever." That's not His desire or His will. We choose.

How much of God do we want? How much do we want to love Him? How much do we want to make His praise glorious and preach the gospel? What kind of faithfulness do we want to show? What kind of zeal do we want to have? It's all up to us. It's our decision and our determination. What do we want?

I personally want my heart and my life to be like the Philadelphians. I want to be part of a community of believers who Jesus looks at and says, "Ya'll have got it going on. I have nothing bad to say. I'm only going to tell you this: open your doors up because people are coming that are going to blow your mind. I can trust you with them. You are going to be blown away on earth, and you're going to be blown away in heaven forever. You are My beloved, and I'm stoked about how you've responded to Me."

Let's get a vision for that kind of living, and let's believe God can impart to us the right heart that the Philadelphian believers had.

God, may You do that in our midst individually. God, may You do that for us corporately.

• • • • • • • • • • • • • • • • •

Part 6

The church at Laodicea

6

PREFACE

We've gone through six letters in which Jesus corrected, comforted, or challenged His churches. We've come to the conclusion that when Jesus challenges or corrects His church, it's never for the purpose of just rubbing their noses in their failure. Jesus doesn't enjoy doing that. If your idea of God is that He is in heaven holding a baseball bat, taking joy in beating us down whenever we make mistakes, then your understanding of God is all wrong. That is not who He is.

He will correct us, but you need to understand why He corrects us—it's because of His unbelievable love for us. He's not doing it just to beat up on us in any way, shape, or form. So in this final letter, if you start to feel challenged or corrected or chastised, remember that He doesn't want to leave you in that spiritual place. He wants you to experience it deeply enough so you'll realize that change has to happen and then respond to His hope and His health. That's why we've gone through these letters over the past weeks—so we could see our need for change and then respond to His hope and health for us.

The seventh and final letter was written to believers in the city of Laodicea. It's my opinion that of all the churches we've studied, this church in Laodicea most reflects the church in the Western world today. Considering the character traits and events associated with the church around the world, I think it'd be fitting for Jesus to address the same message of this letter to much of the Western church, especially the church here in America. I believe there is something for all of us in this letter.

BACKGROUND

The city of Laodicea was a prosperous commercial center. One of their sources of wealth was their famous medical school that was known for a healing eye salve made from Phrygian powder. This salve was named after a former kingdom in an area that is now modern-day Turkey and was probably smeared on eyelids. Occultists used it at the temple of Asclepius, the god of medicine and healing in ancient Greek mythology.

Laodicea was also a clothing manufacturing center and was known for its black wool. The sheep that typically grazed the land produced a soft and rare black wool. Their clothing was very famous and costly.

It's fair to say that Laodicea was a wealthy city whose citizens had a fiercely independent spirit. They refused Roman aid after the earthquake of 60 A.D. and rebuilt the city using their own resources. They had no local water supply since they were an inland city at the crossroads of north-south traffic between Sardis and Perga and east-west traffic from the Euphrates to Ephesus. So they built an aqueduct that ran six miles from the hot springs of Hierapolis to their city. At one point they also gave twenty-two and a half pounds of gold for a temple offering. They were wealthy. They were self-sufficient. They didn't need anybody's help. They were fine on their own . . . or so they thought.

EARLY CONCERNS

In his letter to the Colossians, Paul wrote about the Laodiceans some thirty years before Revelation was written. He said:

> For I want you to know what a great conflict I have for you and those in Laodicea, and for as many as have not seen my face in the flesh, that their hearts may be encouraged, being knit together in love, and attaining to all riches of the full assurance of understanding, to the knowledge of the mystery of

God, both of the Father and of Christ.

Colossians 2:1, 2

Paul had all kinds of anxiety, worry, and trouble related to the believers in Laodicea, and you don't hear Paul talking that way very often. He expressed his hopes for their encouragement, unity, and growth, and he also told them his concerns about them. I think Paul was making a judgment call on the Laodiceans' spiritual state, and it was related to their wealth, all their "stuff," and where they found comfort and security. Paul was saying, "I am troubled for you. Yeah, I want your hearts to be encouraged and knit together in love, but I'm praying for you to attain the riches of the knowledge of God, not just the riches of man's kingdom." It was an apostolic jab from Paul. It was an attention-getter thirty years before Jesus wrote His letter to the church in Laodicea. Paul saw materialistic problems happening. He saw them finding great comfort, security, and affirmation in their wealth. He said, "Here's the deal: you need real wealth. You need to be rich in God." Whew!

If we look at another part of Paul's letter to the Colossians, we find another person who was concerned about the Laodiceans:

> "Epaphras, who is one of you, a bondservant of Christ, greets you, always laboring fervently for you in prayers, that you may stand perfect and complete in all the will of God. For I bear him witness that he has a great zeal for you, and those who are in Laodicea, and those in Hierapolis

Colossians 4:12, 13

Epaphras had great zeal for the Laodiceans. He prayed fervently and passionately that the Laodiceans, even with all of their wealth and all the stuff they thought they had going on, would stand perfect and complete in all the will of God. Epaphras was concerned. Paul was concerned.

Now take a look at Colossians 4:16. When Paul was doing his normal sign-off at the end of the letter, he threw in these instructions:

"Now when this epistle is read among you, see that it is read also in the church of the Laodiceans, and that you likewise read the epistle from Laodicea."

Colossians 4:16

Isn't that interesting? How many of us have the letter to the Laodiceans in our Bibles? None of us do. What happened to that letter the Laodiceans received from Paul and were supposed to share with the Colossians? There are all kinds of funky speculations about it, and I'm going to throw in my ownfunky speculation about it.

Based on what I know about the people in Colossia and what we're going to unpack in Revelation 3, I think the Laodiceans did receive their letter from the apostle Paul. I think it was filled with concerns for their spiritual condition. I think they read it, refused its challenge and correction, crumpled it up, and got rid of it. I think they said, "We don't need to hear this. Nobody else needs to hear this about us either. We don't want anybody reading our mail. We're fine just the way we are. We'll just keep this between us and Paul. This letter is going no further." It's just an idea. I think we could substantiate it with the attitudes the Book of Revelation proves they had. We don't know for sure, but it's certainly possible.

• • • • • • • • • • • • • • • • •

THE MESSAGE TO THE CHURCH AT LAODICEA

Let's read what Jesus had to say to the church of Laodicea in Revelation 3:14–22:

"And to the angel of the church of the Laodiceans write, 'These things says the Amen, the Faithful and True Witness, the Beginning of the creation of God: "I know your works, that you are neither cold nor hot. I could wish you were cold or hot. So then, because you are lukewarm, and neither cold nor hot, I will vomit you out of My mouth. Because you say, 'I am rich, have become wealthy, and have need of nothing'—and do not know that you are wretched, miserable, poor, blind, and naked—I counsel you to buy from Me gold refined in the fire, that you may be rich; and white garments, that you may be clothed, that the shame of your nakedness may not be revealed; and anoint your eyes with eye salve, that you may see. As many as I love, I rebuke and chasten. Therefore be zealous and repent. Behold, I stand at the door and knock. If anyone hears My voice and opens the door, I will come in to him and dine with him, and he with Me. To him who overcomes I will grant to sit with Me on My throne, as I also overcame and sat down with My Father on His throne. He who has an ear, let him hear what the Spirit says to the churches.""'

Revelation 3: 14-22

May we indeed hear anything that God has to say to us in this letter. Let's unpack this, one or two verses at a time.

WHO'S IN CHARGE?

In verse 14, Jesus addressed the church of the Laodiceans,

and the way He did it gives us important information. When you study the Bible, you have to be really meticulous because two little letters or one small word can make all the difference in the world. Here's the deal: when Jesus wrote His letters to Ephesus, Smyrna, Pergamus, Thyatira, Sardis, and Philadelphia, He said, "To the angel of the churches in" and then said the name of the city. This time He said, "To the angel of the church of the Laodiceans."

"So," you ask, "what's the big deal? What was He saying?" He was saying, "This church isn't about the physical, geographic limitations of the city. This isn't about a church that's in a city. This is about a church that has a city in it." This was the church of the Laodiceans. This was the church of the people. This wasn't Jesus' church in a city. This was their church in their city. Jesus wasn't operating this church; the people were.

I find it interesting that the name Laodicea means "decision or rule of the people." They let the very thing that characterized their city creep into their church. The people were in charge there. It's like they said, "This is our decision. We're going to rule this place." And then Jesus said, "This isn't My church; this is your church. You all have taken it over, and you've turned it into something that the gospel and the kingdom of God are not." This was the church of the Laodiceans. The way this letter begins tells us that it was ruled by the people and that Jesus saw it as the people's church, not His church.

Beloved, I've got to tell you something. Anytime a church becomes the church of the people, it's in trouble. Anytime the church says, "Hey, God, we're in charge here. We're going to dictate what is said, when it's said, and how it's said. We're going to just do our own will in this place under the banner and disguise of 'church.' We're just going to do what we want to do and call it 'church.'" When that happens, beloved, it means trouble, trouble, double trouble. Unfortunately, that's what the church at Laodicea was doing. They were in double trouble because they were in charge. They thought they should rule the church because they were wealthy and in need of nothing. Was that really true? They eventually found out they were not.

In verse 14, Jesus also used very strong titles for Himself to establish His authority. He called Himself "the Amen, the Faithful and the True Witness," which means that He is the very foundation of faithfulness and truth. He is the bedrock of all truth, all wisdom, and all faithfulness. Why did He tell them this? To prepare them for what came next. He said, "What I'm about to tell you is based on My truth and My faithfulness to you. You can take this to the bank." He also called Himself "the Beginning of the creation of God." He was telling them that He Himself is the very Word by which the created order came into existence. Jesus was claiming to be nothing less than God in human flesh, and when God speaks we do well to listen, even if we don't like what He has to say or we think we're in charge.

HIS DISMANTLING

After Jesus identified Himself to the church of the Laodiceans, He started lovingly dismantling everything they esteemed—and don't miss that He truly was loving in doing this. He started breaking down everything that they thought made them great in the eyes of the world. Jesus, point by point, started taking those things apart and showing them what He really thought.

Beloved, the simple fact is this: sometimes our lives have to be dismantled before they can be built up, and that's what Jesus did for the church of the Laodiceans. He tore down every idle god. He dismantled everything they thought made them something. He took those things apart piece by piece in order to get those people down to the foundation of faithfulness and truth. Then, their lives could be built up in the image of the Lord Jesus Christ. This is serious stuff.

In the next couple verses, Revelation 3:15, 16, Jesus said,

"I know your works, that you are neither cold nor hot. I could wish you were cold or hot. So then, because you are lukewarm, and neither cold nor hot, I will vomit you out of My mouth."

Revelation 3: 15, 16

There are scholarly arguments about this letter to the church of Laodicea that say it's the only letter in which Jesus had nothing good to say. Some people believe that Jesus had nothing good to say about the church at Sardis as well, but there are a couple of veiled compliments in that letter and we discussed in chapter four. However, when it comes to Laodicea, there's nothing good to be said at all.

Jesus started this letter in the same way He started the other letters by saying, "Hey, I know your works." In past letters, that was followed by different complimentary things, then He lowered the hammer on them and straightened them out, and then He gave them hope again. In this letter, by contrast, Jesus went straight for the jugular. He said, "I know your works, and I've got nothing good to say to you. That's the deal. You're neither cold nor hot, and I wish you were either one or the other. Because you are lukewarm, I will vomit you out of My mouth." Wow!

The church at Laodicea was neither hostile toward nor zealous for the things of God. They were just lukewarm—apathetic, passive, and indifferent. They were just being agreeable, sweet, lovely, and nice. They had the attitude of "Hey, whatever works for you is just fine. Let's all just get along." They were the kind of people with absolutely no passion about anything; they were just existing, not really living. Yet they were supposed to be a church—an assembly of the redeemed of God. They were supposed to be the happiest people around, with the greatest sense of purpose in their lives and the biggest fire in their hearts for the most important cause. However, they preferred a kind of life that was the status quo. Their mantras seemed to be "Business as usual" and "Don't rock the boat."

Let me try to explain what Jesus said about this issue of lukewarmness. He let them know that they were absolutely no different from the tepid, tasteless, lukewarm water from their aqueduct they were so proud of. Remember how they built a water aqueduct? They were pumping water from a hot spring, and by the time it arrived at its location, it was lukewarm, tasteless, and worthless water that had to be thrown out.

Just like that water, their own effort, their own accomplishments, and their own greatness produced nothing of true value. It produced nothing of kingdom value. Jesus has a way of exposing and dismantling the things we so highly esteem and showing that what we think we have is really nothing but a house of cards. He also used words that they understood. They knew exactly what being lukewarm is about. When they'd think of lukewarm water, they'd think, "It's not cool, refreshing, or thirst-quenching. It's not hot for a good cup of coffee or hot tea." They knew exactly what He was saying. He started His dismantling slowly because He loved them.

You can see the tough love in this letter. It was a shocking wake-up call to people who had been bewitched into spiritual slumber by their own abundance of material possessions. Somehow these people bought into the lie that the goal of life is found at the end of the rainbow with the pot of gold—that wealth is the most important thing. It's the mindset that says, "So long as I've got a bunch of money and a bunch of comfort and a bunch of stuff that I like, and I can go wherever I want and buy whatever I want with whoever I want anytime I want. That's it—I've arrived. Is there anything more you could ask for in this life?" Today I am telling you that the answer to that question is, "Yes! There is way more!"

Our problem isn't that we want too much. Our problem is that we're satisfied with too little. We let cash satisfy our hearts. We let the size of our houses satisfy our hearts. We let the size of our bank accounts satisfy our hearts. Hear me: it's not about any of that stuff. It's about knowing God. It's about being rich in His purpose.

I've met enough wealthy people who've looked me in the eyes and said, "It's worth nothing. Yes, it's great to write a check and have luxuries. It's great to be able to help people with your resources. But good night, when your marriage is on the rocks, your kids hate you, you're an alcoholic, you're a workaholic, you don't have peace, and you look at the poor bloke working for minimum wage with a smile on his face as he's pumping gas and you wish you were smiling, too . . . that's troubling." Jesus said to the Laodiceans, "You all have bought a bill of goods here. You are lukewarm because you are looking at things and not at Me." That is tough love.

HIS INDICTMENT

Jesus gave His indictment in verse 17 when He said,

> "You say, 'I am rich, have become wealthy, and have need of nothing'—and do not know that you are wretched, miserable, poor, blind, and naked."
>
> Revelation 3:17

The Laodiceans were completely engulfed in self-sufficient complacency, apathy, and spiritual passivity. They were satisfied all the way into spiritual slumber, so much so that they actually said as members of a church, "We need nothing." Jesus apparently heard that and replied, "You don't need Me? Really? You're in a position in your own kingdom where you don't need God? Oh really?"

I don't know about you, but I think when the Laodiceans read this part of the letter they started feeling nervous. I think the weight of conviction set in on them. Simultaneously they were experiencing the rebuke of God and the loving hand of a correcting Father. Their Father was beckoning them to return to their senses, to turn away from their prodigal lifestyle, and to come home and experience His goodness. Because they said, "We're rich and need nothing," Jesus said, "You guys are missing the boat."

There's a stark contrast between the way they saw themselves and the way Christ saw them in reality. They saw themselves as rich and needing nothing. Jesus saw them as wretched, miserable, poor, blind, and naked. It doesn't get any different than that.

Let me ask you a quick question. I've thought a bunch about lukewarmness and complacency, and I am wondering: how do we get there? How do people get to that place of spiritual slumber?

I think the Laodiceans are a good example of one way you can get there. I think it happens when you see yourself as having arrived and you think you have attained all that there is. You begin to tell yourself, "I'm rich. I'm wealthy. I don't need anything. I've arrived. I've attained." I think that is why Paul wrote a letter to the Laodiceans thirty years earlier and said, "Hey, you need to attain the riches of God, not the riches of man." It begins when we start listening to what the world says, because the world tells us we have to have what everybody wants and what is supposed to bring satisfaction. When we buy into that, then complacency, apathy, and lethargy sets in. All of those things we've attained start having their effect on us and we think, "I've arrived; this is what it's about." That's one way we get to lukewarmness and spiritual slumber.

Another way I believe people get spiritually lukewarm is by convincing their own hearts that the amount of Jesus they have is enough. These people are saying, "Well, maybe I haven't arrived, but I've got enough. I never used to go to church, but now I go to church. I never used to give money, but now I do occasionally. I'm cussing way less than I used to. I don't drink nearly as much. I haven't kicked my dog in six weeks. I'm doing better. I think this is all right for me. I don't want to push it. You know, I don't want to become a Jesus fanatic—like people I've seen in some churches who act like they believe all this stuff." What we have, in this case, is an inoculation of religion that keeps people from Jesus. It's just enough religion to satisfy their spoiled spirits. They believe that they don't need anything more. It's why prayer meetings don't happen, or why they're so sparsely attended. People don't see themselves as desperate for God and needing more of Him.

I've been beating this drum a bunch lately, but we need to keep hearing the beating until we wake up! Our church is in an area with four-plank fences and horses running around—is this heaven or what? The county we're in is supposedly the tenth wealthiest county per capita in the country. Hallelujah! Has our success overcome us? Have we become rich and don't even need God because we can write a check or influence circumstances so they're in our favor?

I want more of God—personally and in the church. I want more of God for me, and I want more of God for you. I know there's the temptation to think, Hey, Berger, look how good you've got it. We are officially a mega church. Wow! We've arrived! We've got mega church status. We've got mega people. We've got mega offerings. We've got mega problems. We've got mega whatever, but we're mega!

The question is, do we have mega life? Do we have mega Jesus? Are there mega miracles? Is there mega sanctification? Is there mega memorization of Scripture? Are people beating the doors down to get to prayer meetings and Bible studies? Until those things can be described as mega, there is more to be had. I'm going to preach this vision and keep pushing for it and believing it can happen, despite our wealth and mega this or that. The Laodiceans thought they had arrived, and they had a totally different view of themselves than Jesus had of them.

It is a sobering word for those who are supposed to be clean in Christ's righteousness to be told they are miserable and wretched. They were supposed to be rich in Christ's kingdom treasures, and yet He told them they were poor. They were supposed to be seeing Christ's inexhaustible glories, and yet He said, "You all are blind." They were supposed to be clothed in Christ's righteousness, and yet He told them they were naked. Wow!

HIS COUNSEL

After giving His indictment, Jesus gave them counsel. He

said,

> "I counsel you to buy from Me gold refined in the fire, that you may be rich; and white garments, that you may be clothed, that the shame of your nakedness may not be revealed; and anoint your eyes with eye salve, that you may see"
>
> Revelation 3:18

In the first statement, Jesus was messing with their gold and what they had given in the past. He was messing with what they thought was important—cash and possessions and everything else. So He didn't only point out their lukewarm spiritual condition and lukewarm water; He also poked at their gold. He said, "I want you to get from Me gold refined in the fire." Gold refined in the fire is nothing less than deep-seated Christian character that is forged and purged in the fires of Christ's presence. He takes our submitted lives and plunges us into the blast furnace of His presence, so we can be purified. The dross, the scum that forms on the surface of molten metal, rises to the top and He scrapes it off. He puts us through the fire and through the pruning so we can become people of deeper character and we won't be just shallow, materialistic "Ken and Barbie" look-alikes.

Jesus said, "I want you to buy gold refined in the fire. I don't want you to get up from the altar, the living altar of sacrifice, every time I start doing a work in your life. Every time I start to prune you in the vineyard of the Lord, I don't want you to run the other way. I want you to buy gold refined in the fire. I want you to have a true, deep Christian character and experience My transforming power in Your life. I want you to be able to say to God with genuine sincerity, 'O God, may Your will be worked in my life regardless of the cost, regardless of the temperature of the fire, regardless of the size of the pruning shears that cut me back, so that I can bear more fruit.'" He's talking about real Christianity, not the Laodiceans' church stuff. He's talking about the real deal.

In the second part of His counsel, He basically said: "I want you to get some white garments. Be clothed in holiness and righteousness. I don't want you to walk around spiritually naked." Isn't this a sight for sore eyes? I wonder what it would look like if we could see each other spiritually. What would we see if we saw each other in our spiritual clothes? Maybe we would be shocked and say, "Oh! Put something on!" Or maybe we would say, "Wow! Look at the clothing, the splendor, the purity, the holiness, and the character of God that person is walking in."

Jesus said, "I want you to have white garments. I want you to be clothed in holiness and righteousness." Remember what they were so proud of wearing? It was black wool. Jesus said, "I know the black wool fascinates you. I know you're happy that it's sold on Madison Avenue and that all the fancy stores and celebrities have it, but it stinks in My nostrils! It's polluted with the corruption of this world. What I want for you is a white garment, not the fanciness of the world or the fashion of the day. People, replace your black wool with My white garments."

The third part of His counsel was that they should anoint their eyes with eye salve so they might see. Now what did He mean by that? I think He was saying, "You all are so big on using your fancy eye salve; you think you're going to improve your-selves and make yourselves see better. Well, it ain't cutting it. You need to anoint your eyes with My eye salve. Forget the Phry-gian eye ointment you think so highly of." Jesus said they needed to start seeing their true spiritual condition through the truth and faithfulness of the Word of God and stop settling for their own spiritual delusion. He wanted them to anoint their eyes and then take a hard look at themselves.

Sometimes when we look long enough at the reality of who we are, it can be very discouraging, especially when we look into the light and the truth of God's Word. We read scriptures like this letter to the Laodiceans, and then we start to look inside and think, "Oh, I don't like what I see. God's truth has exposed some-thing in me that I've known is wrong and ungodly. I've had just enough of Jesus in me to say, 'Oh Lord, don't look there. Don't see that. I don't want to see that. Can we dress it up with some black wool? Do something to beautify it; make it pretty. I don't want to go there.'"

Listen, we need to go there and listen to this counsel. We need to do a real checkup. Nobody has to play games or try to impress anybody. Everybody has work to do and areas to grow, right? So are we doing it? That's the bigger question. Not just saying, "Yeah. Amen. That's right, I've got room to grow. I'm not perfect." The real question is: what are we doing about it? Don't stay there looking at the failures. Recognize them, and then do something about it. Jesus said, "Buy some gold refined in My fire, put on some white clothes, and put My ointment on your eyes that will help you see truth."

HIS HOPE

I'm sure at this point in reading the letter, the Laodiceans were feeling embarrassed and ashamed. I'm sure everyone gulped and thought, Oh man. As only Jesus could do, He took them to that low point and then offered them hope, just like He offers us hope today.

The hope is found in verse 19 when Jesus said,

"As many as I love, I rebuke and chasten. Therefore be zeal-ous and repent." He was saying, "I know I'm being hard on you all, but desperate times call for desperate measures. You all are so sleepy and so dead and so out of touch with spiritual reality, I had no choice but to kick the door down and slap you across the face to wake you up. I'm doing it because I love you and I'm not willing to let you stay the way you are. Can you hear Me? As many as I love, I rebuke and I chasten."

Revelation 3:19

I love the fact that I can feel conviction from Christ. It means I'm His. Hebrews 12:8 says, "If you are without chasten-ing . . . then you are illegitimate and not sons." I love the fact that as I'm preaching, my own heart is convicted by the Spirit of God, who is saying, "Berger, I am calling for change, but I am also giving hope."

Jesus also told them they needed to be zealous and repent. I love the order of those words. This was the solution to the problem in the Laodicean church: they needed to be zealous and they needed to repent. They couldn't be lukewarm and just agree with everything. They couldn't be lukewarm and say, "Sure, that makes sense" to whatever they heard. They couldn't be lukewarm and say, "Well, that was better than last week." They had to be zealous, and they had to repent.

Zealousness means that you don't wait for the fourth verse or the chorus before you come to the altar. You are zealous when you think, I've heard from God. He's given me hope. He's not content with just spewing me out of His mouth. He's offering me solutions. He's offering me health and hope. He's offering forgiveness and mercy. Man, when I heard what Jesus was offering me, I was like Speedy Gonzales, going right to the front and bending down at the altar to say, "Oh God, I don't know how I became the way I am. I got sucked into the world's ways of doing things. Somehow I became spiritually complacent and now I'm lukewarm. I'm not against You, but I'm not for You. I'm here to admit it. I'm sorry that I've confessed Your name and lived in spiritually shallow places. I am repenting of that. Today, right now, I'm responding to You zealously. Please touch my heart. Work in my life."

I want to tell you something that we get wrong sometimes. We want to comfort people before they've mourned. Jesus said, "Blessed are those who mourn, for they shall be comforted" (Matt. 5:4). It's right for us to see ourselves how we really are and say, "Jesus, I am sorry," with tears coming down our faces. It's wrong for us to say, "Oh no, no, don't get off of that seat. No, Jesus forgives. No, put a smile on your face and go back to your seat." Jesus said the ones who mourn are blessed and will be comforted. He said we should wake up and be zealous. We should get red hot about one thing: repentance. When repentance comes, then real life change will come.

HIS KNOCK

Jesus said in the next verse,

> "Behold, I stand at the door and knock. If anyone hears My voice and opens the door, I will come in to him and dine with him, and he with Me"
>
> Revelation 3:20

Jesus was knocking at the door. Jesus was asking the Laodicean church, "Are you listening? Have I lost you yet? Come on, pay attention. I'm outside knocking. Are you there? I am near you, but I'm still outside. I'm within knocking distance, but I'm still outside. So I'm knocking. Will you hear Me knocking on your heart? Will you open the door and let Me come in?"

I think it's amazing that in the last letter, Jesus opened the door for the church at Philadelphia, and in this letter to the church at Laodicea Jesus asked, "Will you open the door for Me?"

Here's the thing: He wasn't angry. He wasn't irate. He was saying, "Will you please respond? Have you heard? I want in. I want to dine with you, and I want you to dine with Me. I want us to have an intimate and beautiful relationship. It's only going to happen if you are zealous and repent. I'm standing at the door knocking."

HIS PROMISE

Jesus gave them a great promise at the end of the letter:

> "To him who overcomes I will grant to sit with Me on My throne, as I also overcame and sat down with My Father on His throne"
>
> Revelation 3:21

Jesus said, "You Laodiceans have been ruling yourselves and the people; you sit on your own thrones. If you want to sit on a true throne, come with Me and sit on My throne. In order to do that, however, you'll have to get rid of your own thrones first. You've got to give them up. Surrender them to Me."

You cannot keep being in charge of your own life and call Him Lord at the same time. That's a contradiction. We need to go from Jesus only being the Savior of our sins to Him being the Lord, the Master and Ruler of our actions. We need to be submitted to Him.

Without question, Jesus had a word for these guys that was sobering; but at the same time, His message was full of hope, full of promise, and full of a future. He dismantled everything they thought was so great and then said, "It's all about Me, and you're welcome. I want you. Let Me in, and I'll let you in. Get rid of your thrones—they're not really that big of a deal anyway—and come sit with Me on My throne."

REPENT AND OPEN THE DOOR TO JESUS

Are you lukewarm? Has something happened in your heart that has made you like the Laodiceans in any way? Do you need to repent? You might not be in some disgusting sin. That's not the issue here; He doesn't rebuke them for that. He rebukes them for not being into anything. He rebukes them for being lukewarm and passive.

What does your heart look like? What's going on? Are you hungry for God? Are you hungry for prayer? Are you hungry for worship? These questions came up when we studied the letter to the church at Sardis. Are you hungry for those things? Do they have priority in your life? Man, if they do not, I don't know what else to say except that you should just be honest about it, ask Him to forgive you, and be zealous for it.

Right now, why don't you give Jesus the present of your heart? Let it be broken and repentant and determined to walk with Him in genuine sincerity and passionate zeal for the rest of your days. You can do that today, right now, while you are reading this. Don't wait! If God has spoken to your heart, if He has knocked on the door to your heart, I don't care whether or not you've ever answered an altar call—respond to Him! I'm probably talking to people who have never answered an altar call because they think it's too fanatical. Be zealous and repent; let's make this right today. Let's acknowledge that we hear Jesus speaking truth through the Word, agree with Him, and respond to Him in obedience right now.

I'm not trying to appeal to your emotions. I'm not trying to make you respond out of guilt. I'm here saying that if Jesus has spoken to your spirit and you know that change needs to happen, then take this time to pray to Him about it. Ask Him to work in your heart and life.

The Scripture says, "If you will hear His voice: 'Do not harden your hearts, as in the rebellion'" (Ps. 95:7, 8). Maybe your heart's pounding out of your chest. Maybe you're reading this and you've never met Christ in a personal way. Maybe you've been religious, but you know in your heart that it's empty and you're still searching for something real.

His name is Jesus, and what He offers is salvation—right now. It's free. He loves you.

• • • • • • • • • • • • • • • • •

NOTES

CHAPTER 1: EPHESUS

1. Leonard Ravenhill, *Why Revival Tarries*, (C) 1979, Bethany House Publishers

CHAPTER 2: SMYRNA

1. C.S. Lewis, *The Problem of Pain*, © 1940, C.S. Lewis Pte. Ltd. Copyright restored © 1996 C.S. Lewis
Pte. Ltd.

CHAPTER 3: PERGAMOS AND THYATIRA

1. An epidemiological study from Vancouver, Canada of data tabulated between 1987 and 1992 for AIDS-related deaths reveals that male homosexual or bisexual practitioners lost up to 20 years of life expectancy. The study concluded that if 3 percent of the population studied were gay or bisexual, the probability of a 20-year-old gay or bisexual man living to 65 years was only 32 percent, compared to 78 percent for men in general. R. S. Hogg, S. A. Strathdee, et al., "Modeling the Impact of HIV Disease on Mortality in Gay and Bisexual Men," *International Journal of Epidemiology*, 26(3): 657-661, p. 659

2. Virtue, David W. "*The Body's Grace: Sex According to Rowan Williams.*" http://listserv.virtueonline.org/pipermail/virtueonline_listserv.virtueonline.org/2002-September/004129.html.

CHAPTER 5: PHILADELPHIA

1. Ishmael was Abraham's first son. Impatient to have a son, Abraham's wife, Sarah, offered her handmaiden, Hagar, to Abraham. She conceived and bore Ishmael. Hagar and Ishmael later left Abraham
and Sarah to live in the desert of Paran.

www.ingramcontent.com/pod-product-compliance
Lightning Source LLC
Chambersburg PA
CBHW071559040426
42452CB00008B/1232